P

M000202460

Sex, Drugs, and Rocking Code is highly recommended to those misfits who planned to use their eccentricity to innovate apps, programs, society, companies, and businesses but still don't know how. What we need is a great example to follow or to learn from, such as this daring book here. Not a single minute wasted reading this. It's awe-inspiring, thought-provoking, enriching—not to mention very funny. Do yourself a favor, read it anywhere, and take yourself for a wild ride!

Lisa Cloutier | owner, The Islander Inn, Montana

It's never boring from start to finish. It hooked me up! There's this long, captivating section in the book about boredom and the gifts it can bring! It's amazing to learn how to channel such boredom and translate it into solid hours of productive work. Highly recommended to everyone, especially to the bored young ones out there questioning their life and career choices!

Chip Baker | founder, Cultivate Colorado

Sometimes I spend time with this book before starting my day—to get into the flow or the zone. The author talks a lot about the concept of flow and teaches us a couple of ways to get there. I find that most helpful to me, for I value my time! Time not spent *in flow* is time not well spent, as I learned from here. That's just one of the dozens of insights this book offers. The sooner you read this book, the better.

Chris Catranis | CEO, Babylon Telecommunications; best-selling author of *Disruptive Leadership*

i

What's apparent here is the author's daring and drive to forward himself and the world. His story hits us like a powerful energy drink. That's what the book does to me; it awakens me thoroughly. It's also a reinvigorating read especially when you're a workaholic like the author—grinding for sixteen hours a day. The book is superbly good company for me, also for you.

Rick Orford | co-founder & executive producer, Travel Addicts Life; bestselling author of *The Financially Independent Millennial*

This book is so good. I thought I'd flick through it. Thirty minutes should do it. Easy. Wrong. I had to cancel the next two meetings. I was hooked. I read half the book in one sitting, then finished it that night. It's unlike anything you've read before. You'll get a laugh reading it. And you might just start to see the world differently. And what that means for you. Which is probably a big deal. Read it!

Mike Rhodes | founder & CEO, WebSavvy

Author Paul W. Carter has crafted a superb tale that features a life fully lived, and it offers many different levels of entertainment for its readers. For fans of autobiographical writing, the narrative quality is honest and raw. Carter delivers a frank perspective that is laced with both wry humor and laugh-out-loud, outrageous moments, balancing some tender moments about how one approaches life alongside the mishaps and adventures which we can all relate to.

K. C. Finn for Readers' Favorite

When I first started reading the preface of *Sex, Drugs, and Rocking Code*, I laughed out loud, and I thought it was going to be a humorous collection of personal anecdotes. Although the personal stories are hilarious at times, there are really profound messages throughout this well-written memoir. I resonated so much with the author regarding fitting into society's idea of normality and trying to find your unique voice in a world that conditions you to conform.

Lesley Jones for Readers' Favorite

You know when you've been thinking about something but don't think anybody else sees things that way until the moment you pick up a book and read your random thoughts explained in a way that makes so much sense? That's exactly how I felt when I read *Sex, Drugs, and Rocking Code*. Paul W. Carter's musings are ones everyone can relate to. However, *Sex, Drugs, and Rocking Code* is for readers that can take a joke and don't get offended easily. If that's you, prepare for a really good laugh at Paul W. Carter's wild tales, but amazingly, Paul gives some really profound notes on every one of his experiences. I had a fantastic read and will definitely be making use of the burnout process.

Foluso Falaye for Readers' Favorite

Sex DRUGS AND ROCKING CODE

The Uncensored Autobiography
of an Anonymous Programmer

By
Paul W. Carter

CP

ISBN (pbk) 978-1-943386-96-3
ISBN (ebook) 978-1-943386-95-6

Library of Congress Control Number: 2020913427

Contents

Preface

Breadth-first search (BFS)

You should read this book if you feel you don't belong in the normal world, which coincidentally applies to almost everybody, but we'll circle back on that later. You probably shouldn't read this book if you're easily offended. If you're a judgmental dick and generally ignorant, then I can promise that this book isn't for you. If you're well-adjusted and happy in a normal society, then this book probably won't be a good use of your time either, because you can't get that time back.

So why should you read this book? Normally, we follow somebody who has the things we want. Maybe you always wanted to be a cool kid, but one day, you realized that the things cool kids had weren't the things you truly wanted. We realize soon enough that most of the people telling us what we should do don't have what we want. Why would we follow their advice when we realize "Well, I don't want to live *there*" or "But I don't want to do *that*"?

Most of us are scrambling to figure things out and find someone to follow. We want to find our tribe and know where we fit in and with whom we fit in. But some of us will not find the other weirds, so we must find our own flow—the kind of flow where you're so focused on one thing the rest of the world disappears. You're slightly detached, and maybe even quite detached, from reality. You have that confidently awkward, almost *Asperger'sesque,* vibe.

Find the minimum depth of a binary tree.

A girl I was in love with once told me flat out, "You're pretty good-looking and smart, but you're an eccentric, and I'd rather be with somebody else." She left me to go date trashier guys. But hey, that's what she wanted, and who's to say what a Trash Panda is or isn't?

Sometimes I think it'd be much better to be normal than smart, but then I'd have to work harder. So I accept that I'm an eccentric, a contradiction, a mad scientist, and sometimes a dick. If that sounds like you, then read on. You'll be able to relate.

I'm not specifically talking to the young coders and engineers, but frankly, the weirdos. It's for those of you who develop Stockholm syndrome around the BS that's made for everybody but fits nobody. You don't have to be a coder, an engineer, or a nerd to find value in my words. It has nothing at all to do with your field. You could be a rapper, sports ballplayer, or an artist.

Reverse an array without affecting special characters.

No matter your choice, follow your dreams, but you must train yourself to do something profitable.

Being a rapper is a great dream, and it works out for some. Being a music producer is a great career that puts you in places you want to be, and maybe a dream happens. But if it doesn't work out, you don't want to be unhappy while you whittle your life away at Starbucks. You won't end up in a lifetime service job or selling drugs if you have a backup plan you can mold. Just don't let your dreams impede your *dreams*.

My goal is to inspire people not to become service workers while chasing their true desires. Sometimes you might be nomadic once you figure out that a paycheck is a safety net created for the weak—a security blanket if you lack the heart to choose something scary while still having safety. Choose a career or something to do that will set you up to have the lifestyle you want. Having a safe analog or parallel path to your dream makes sense, doesn't it?

That's my roundabout way of saying everybody's a weirdo, so this book should appeal to everybody—including the fifty-year-old dude who says, "Oh man, I wish I could do what you do!" To him, I say, "Well, you can. You've got twenty years of experience. Why can't you do what I do?"

Then I hear the excuses. I'm not saying there won't be suffering, but you can have whatever you want, although you may not know what you want yet.

Merge a linked list into another linked list at alternate positions.

I took a silly test when I was a kid, and I was told I could be a Nobel Peace Prize winner or some other such nonsense. Obviously, I didn't take that path because I partied too hard. Problem solved. But I'm a failure, a winner, a complete, utter contradiction. But then who isn't? Unfortunately, or fortunately, I may have taken it to the extreme.

I find life to be a joke, so I may as well laugh at it. I was once told I was not a Jack-of-all-trades yet a master-of-all-trades, and that was confusing. I'm a cocky asshole, and part of that is because everything has come rather easily for me. Well, except being bored or stable. If you can relate, we'll be talking about the gifts that boredom can bring.

You'll see that I don't like to waste time on thrills, being PC, or being *woke*, as the kids say. In the right room, I'll be woke, but if you ask me, that's why nothing gets done. We're too worried about other people getting butthurt about words. I'm blunt to a fault, and I give nearly zero fucks about insecurities because I already dealt with most of mine, and the remainder I've accepted.

You can call me whatever you want. You can say whatever you want. It's not my problem. I have shit to build. I have no interest in tap-dancing on the razor blades afoot. If you want to be a failure, wallow in your weakness, but do it somewhere else. My great-grandmother told me something I will never forget. She said that being mature doesn't mean acting like an adult all the time—it's knowing when to do so.

Introduction

Written in Technicolor. Read this in monotone.

There will always be men killing each other for what feels like nothing to a good many of us. They may be glorified as gods or utterly demonized. But there will always be men who become nothing, and the world will never notice them. There will always be men fighting for what feels right—what is close to home and important to them—and they may be glorified as leaders or brushed aside by the masses as a radical, or as a nothing.

Then there are those of us that kill ourselves without even meaning to—those of us that build the conveniences you take for granted and find time in your "busy" lives to complain about at great length. We are chasing something your grandmother thinks is greed, but she has no idea what it is, and neither do you.

Yet.

The interesting thing about the world—the thing often missed—is that you don't know what would have become *if* something else had happened. It's very easy to say that your way would have worked in the event of failure, but you don't know *if* it would or would not have in all reality, because it did not happen.

There are nerds and rock stars, and then there is the mistake called "me" in between. This is the story of when code leaks into your rock star life, and you end up in rock star purgatory with all the mistakes and none of the fame.

```
int INTRODUCTION()

{

    if (TRUE == liar)

    {
```

Do you know what it feels like to wake up every morning and want more?

I sure do.

"Don't you have enough money?" says the brown-eyed beauty sitting on the edge of the bed as she brushes the tears from below her high cheekbone. Tears, man, they're tears staining her perfectly tanned skin.

"It's not about the money, it's about creating something. It's about doing something you didn't think was possible and, frankly, wasn't possible until you had done it." I'm sure I'm not making it any better.

I'm not lying. It's not about the money, the tangible things, the power, or the respect. No, it's about getting more time buried alive in *the zone*. Like a drug, it eats at me if I don't spend a good amount of time every day 100 percent focused on something. Anything. I don't care—be it writing software, creating graphics, making my own organic chapstick, chopping motorcycles, building lamps.

The list goes on and on.

How am I to tell her that I love her silky brown legs that go on for days, but our conversations usually end up with me imagining complex, nonexistent data structures? How do I say that I love the way her smile lights up a room, but I don't see it often enough to remember it when she's gone?

"I feel like I'm not a priority to you," she whimpers in a delicate mix of desperation and what can only be anger.

True.

You're not. It's nothing personal, except that it's completely personal.

I blurt something to the effect of "Of course you are!"

False.

Liar.

But I don't stop. I continue, "I'm just trying to build a future for us, and that requires sacrifice for both of us."

True, maybe.

Probably time to stop talking. I'm quickly creeping out the Boolean territory.

Nope. I spit out, "I love you, boo, but you're stressing me out."

True.

Seriously, bud. Stop now. Leave before this gets worse. Without stopping, "You're being selfish. Do you know how much work this has been? And you're worried about priorities?"

```
>> sigsegv: Segmentation Fault
#ifndef HAVE_SIGSEGV_RECOVERY

   CrashAndBurn(); // We have no way to recover

#endif
```

Her eyes turn to fire. "Leave."

I told myself that two sentences ago. I should have stopped two sentences early on about every thought I have. That would stifle a bit of the whole "letting out just how terribly selfish I am" thing.

It's a life spent drowning in myself. Pushing people away because they eat my precious time to be with myself, time to be inside something. Then when the social silence begins to creep at the edges of my vision, I find it's time to be inside someone. Short-term love requires very little patience but fills the void for only a short time. Long-term love requires a whole lot of being utterly bored. That person becomes a reflection upon me, and their failings are a significant bother.

Flings become the patch to the bug that tears my life apart. A patch for the all-encompassing feeling that if someone loves me, the challenge is gone. If they don't, then I can just tear myself to pieces trying to figure out why. A fling means two weeks of the good part of a relationship—the beginning. Then nothing, space, silence, the option to do whatever I want all the time.

If I can't be with someone or just wasn't feeling it, I can always find a way to escape from reality. A night of tetrahydrocannabinol and ethanol, with an emphasis on benzoylmethylecgonine, can make me forget that I just came up for air and things are dire and empty.

I could get drunk and stoned, high on cocaine. For tonight, I'm not sure alcohol is in order. A quick stop at the 7-11 ATM bearing the redundant ATM Machine" sticker and I'm off to Jah's to pitch in on a night of skiing on white powder and the burning of "green sweaters" (noodle on switching adjective order). It's almost like I'm twenty-two years old again.

I wonder where it will all end.

```
    }

    return FAIL;

}
```

I

Human Principles

Love

Though being single is great, it's not.

Love is a conundrum. You crave it, yet it makes you boring and dull. How do you find the balance between love and boredom? The goal is to strike a balance between needing love and its accompanying nuisances and being alone with its accompanying nuisances—because both existences have caveats. With maturity, you learn to select the one that makes the most sense for you and accept what comes with it.

Learn to fill your resulting boredom with strong strife as strife removes boredom. Why strife? Because when we have an always perfectly good life, nothing stands out. Nothing feels that great. If you're going to five-star dinners every night, with no contrast, those dinners become average. There's nothing to compare them to. And since there's not a ten-star dinner, you're screwed, life's fucked.

Love leads you to waste time and money, it's very inefficient—but so is being alone.

Invariably, in relationships, you have a lot of stupid conversations ad nauseam, and within the first sentence, you know what the next hour of your life will look like. So why do you engage in the process? Well, because somebody has to get their feelings out. Aww, shit. That provides for unending, boring-ass conversations.

But seven and a half billion people across the globe are having these very same discussions, so you're not doing anything new or different. You're technically wasting time, just like everybody else. Everybody on earth has the "You're not paying enough attention to me!" conversation.

The question is what to do about it.

Being alone drives you to the ends of the earth to fill this void you can't explain. You do a lot of drugs or traveling and still end up wasting time and money. That freedom is awesome, but it carries the same caveats as being in love. Freedom can bore too.

Life as a human means you have to balance love versus no love for those who are insane like me. But don't give up on love, even though it's a waste of time. Without it, you drive yourself even crazier and waste your time anyway. So if love is a balancing act between being single and being with someone, how do you know which side of that divide is best?

You need to try everything and learn your likes and dislikes.

You may think you hate tomatoes, but maybe you haven't tried roasting them. Tomatoes could be good. Somebody likes them, so they have to be good in some incarnation. Similarly, it makes sense to go into situations with an open mind and try different things. For example, I've never had a type. I've dated people from different races, backgrounds, and careers. I've tried *to try* every iteration of a girlfriend, and after a while, I learned what I do and don't like.

I had a buddy who got a phone number from a girl, and then he said, "I'm not calling her. She's just a waitress."

No, she's a person who waits tables. Have an open mind, and know that all people are new experiences. Don't think they're not hot, smart, or successful enough for you. Learn who a person is before you judge. Dig deeper. Anytime you feel judgment, swallow it because it's stupid and wrong. You can judge a group as stereotypes are a great first order characteristic, but they're for people, not individuals.

Love for an individual has never been a guiding principle for me; maybe I'm lucky like that. My love for my work and the community at large is why I'm driven to do what I do, but my love for an individual has been primarily sad and depressing. In my introduction, I laid out how things go for me. I don't connect well with a single human, but I would rather see the betterment of everybody. So love has never become a guiding principle, and further, I hope it never will be.

The Greeks spent an inordinate amount of time thinking on love.

Let's say that you have to love what you do, love your life, and love the people in your life, so let's get the definitions out of the way. Going down another level, the type of love you have for each thing matters. For this section, I'm deferring to the Greeks and will offer a basic conversation because we'd need weeks to understand the depth of the Greek words for love.

When we say love, we're generally talking about how Kanye loves Kim, but there are many degrees of love. Although the Greeks defined different kinds of love, I'll focus on eros, philia, and agape. Eros is the sex and romance side of things, philia is the brotherly/sisterly love of things, and agape is the selfless love.

Here are my thoughts…

Eros is known as the love of the body.

Eros can be a problem as it blinds us, and you can do (and most likely have done) profoundly stupid things in the name of eros. You can make poor decisions. Why? Because you don't use logic when you use your genitals. It's like the blood can only flow to one head: they're two entirely different thought processes.

When you feel small, you might fill that void with eros. When you feel large, you can use eros to emasculate others. Interestingly enough, most people think empires fall over love, but it's usually not love, but lust. Lust puts blinders on your eyes and takes the focus from loving humanity in an agape sense to the selfish place where eros is driving the bus.

Let's talk about the dangers of eros.

In all things, you need to identify the weakness you feel. You have to know when you're feeling it and have the maturity to know when you're deciding with your lower brain. When you discover that's the case, you should probably not.

I don't consider lust to be love. Lust is an immature excitement; it's hormones, a chemical interaction. When you feel lust, it doesn't mean you truly care about the person. You could, as both love and lust could exist, but when unchecked, eros can be frightening.

We all have lustful feelings. But you have to know when to act. Think logically about your decision, and determine if it's still a good idea, even though eros is in charge. Being aware of your feelings is important, so you can make an informed decision about whether you're feeling lust or love. Check with yourself, and make sure not to act too impulsively.

However, the lustful eros love can come in handy; that type of love of what you do seems to make you more successful over being correct. Say you go into a job interview and—surprise and shocker alert—they ask you, "Why do you want to work here?"

Since you answer every question correctly because you're after a job, you say what you think you should say: "Well, I want a solid paycheck, and I want to work hard to advance the company's end goals."

Fuck that. That never works out.

Compare that answer to "I want to work here because I fucking *love* building stuff."

This is the difference between loving what you do and loving the external rewards for showing up. When you have a har-on for what you do, you go much further. If you're doing the thing because it's a good career or a paycheck, you're lost in puppy love, and you will not be good at what you do. Also, most people will be able to pick up on that.

Instead of working some mundane career and frowning every day when you go to work, you wake up smiling as you think, *I love what I do!*

Philia is the affectionate love between friends.

Philia usually exists between equals. You feel affectionate toward others and see everyone around you as an equal. It doesn't mean you think we're equally skilled or equally blessed but rather we all have the same feelings and capacity for being human and being good.

I believe that philia is where you should live. You should love and respect everyone, but you don't have to like everybody. But if you will make a choice based on any kind of love, I feel that philia is most closely linked to logic.

Humans often take shortcuts and use stereotypes. Understand that we can be selfish. While people are stupid, individuals are not. We all make mistakes, and no one is better than somebody else. We might be broke today and rich tomorrow, and it doesn't matter.

Put yourself in situations to understand how other people live, but you have to be cold sometimes. It's difficult to put yourself out and look for the good. If you say something like Thanos from *Avengers* did, "Half of the world has to disappear," then you accept that you could be part of that half that need not be around.

Agape love is selfless, spiritual love.

The Greeks strove to find agape love in all things above all else. But agape is a double-edged sword. As soon as you "know" something, you ignore everything to the contrary. That's how agape love can be used as a tool for ignorance.

Let's show agape love of country. Go talk to a strong political supporter, and you'll find out they "know" what's right for the world, but they couldn't tell you *why* it's right. Rarely do I hear a political supporter say, "Her tax plans around capital gains are wonderful for the country." Or "It makes sense for the trade embargoes because it's forcing Americans to innovate and work and find ways within the country to cycle money."

Let's leave politics and talk about religion. For example, your faith means science can't be right while science means your faith is wrong. Both positions are ignorant. If you have an all-powerful God who can use any tool to create, then no tool used for creation can disprove God.

Screw you, Bill Nye and Mr. Ham! I used to love Bill Nye, and now I can't stand him because he tried to disprove God with science. Ham tried to disprove science with God. I think they're both idiots. This kind of agape love for blind adherence creates more hate and violence than anything else. Agape love is a crutch for ignorance.

I don't want to say I don't have faith, but I don't have faith in the interpretations of humans through this type of love. The love of God can blind you, and it's important to be wary of this and particularly of other people's interpretations. There's nothing wrong with loving your God, but there is something wrong with blind faith in anything, so always ask questions.

There should be no point at which you take something that anybody tells you as 100 percent truth.

People are software.

You're a system, and your software has to follow guidelines for things to work well. You must have the same way of handling situations. A computer is a linear time-independent (LTI) system, but people are not. You give a computer the same input, and every time, it'll provide the same output.

With humans, the same input at a different time will produce a different result, because we are non-LTI systems. If your programming or template aligns with another, you'll have a lot more agreement. Agreeing on one point is cool. When you first meet somebody, you're like, "Oh my gosh, we both like the same music. You like avocados? I fucking *love* avocados."

You'll find all kinds of weird little things you have in common, but since you do a hundred billion things, you can always find things in common with another. What's important is seeing over time if you have the same outputs.

Make sure you want that union and not that person—because that makes the person an object. Do you want that union because it's right for both of you? Do you align? Do you build each other up? Are you constructive interference sine waves that are in phase and build each other up and multiply? Or are you destructive interference, which is when sine waves are 180 degrees out of phase and destroy each other?

Constructive versus destructive interference.

Constructive interference is when two build each other up; your sign waves are aligned, and you add up, and you're now double. Yet everybody can be out of phase; we all have our different phase angles, and you'll always have harmonics or distortions because nobody is perfectly aligned. But what you want to do is minimize those distortions so that they can be cleaned or they aren't underdamped or runaway.

I was head-over-heels in love with my ex-fiancé Tara—I loved her to death. We had an interesting relationship that led us to meet in different parts of the country. I think we met in ten cities before she ever saw where I lived. We moved in together, and when we settled in, we realized we hadn't done the right things earlier. We'd been so blinded by the initial excitement, and then we realized we'd wasted a lot of time in the wrong relationship.

Tara and I got in an argument at one point because I said, "I would want my kids to respectfully question everything."

She said, "You never question an elder." That's one of those software programming things that will repeatedly rear its ugly head.

"Does that mean that anytime somebody in a position of power tells you to do something, you're going to do it?" I asked. "That's going to be a problem. What if my boss is an idiot, why would I do what he says?"

"Well, you should listen to him. It's the hierarchy."

"I'm not going to listen to him. I'm going to quit."

"Then you're an idiot. The boss is the boss."

That belief is a template, and when you're in a relationship, your templates need to line up. I'm not saying Tara's belief is wrong, but that it doesn't align with my beliefs. As to who is correct, we'll figure it out when we're dead or we won't. Either the atheists or the religious people are right. I'm hoping the atheists are wrong, but we'll see when we get to the end.

When you have qualms over a certain situation, you should already be close enough to each other in deciding how to handle a thing. You need to line up software between people. Find someone who is not so similar but shares enough templates or values that the two of you will have less conflict inherently. Otherwise, you will continually destructively interfere.

Everything is a wave, a cycle. You will do the same thing repeatedly no matter what. Every situation is a repeat of another with some mild changes. If you interfere every time that sine wave hits, it will keep happening, and every time, it will get a little worse. No one is perfect, and no one is the same as you are, but pay attention.

When you're talking to each other, listen; you can't just hear the other person's stories of childhood. Listen and think about how they responded to that situation and how you would respond to that situation. Put yourself in their shoes with the other factors. If they've been abused and so they ran away, but you've never been abused, then do your best to understand their mindset so you can understand why they ran away.

It comes down to listening, not only hearing. You're not chatting with the person to create bonds. You're using conversation to see if, logically, the two of you would do nearly the same things. Would you respect their decisions at a given moment? We do illogical things or let ourselves suffer because our partner has illogical feelings, and that's the other side of that love we all have. We waste time tap-dancing on eggshells because of our understanding of love.

You can't hear as if it's just a story. You have to listen to how their software responded. When you tell a story, they should do the same. You're building that relationship, and you're growing; you're interfacing with each other. If those interfaces don't line up, data is going to hit bounds, and it will be a mess.

Keep your eyes open. Not to take this to a crude place, but if you're staring at somebody's tits, you're not learning anything about them. You're objectifying them, and that's a problem. If somebody asks if you're a T-man or an A-man, you should be able to say, "I'm a P-man—a personality man. I want to make sure our sine waves are in sync."

Most guys don't understand when they're on the younger side that no matter what a woman looks like, she will be beautiful to you when you love her. Women figure that out young, while men in their fifties look back at old relationships and say, "Ah, crap. I sure messed that one up."

Tara, oh, Tara.

I've been engaged twice, and Tara was my second fiancé. With the explosion at the end of the relationship, I realized at that moment that I had been blind before. And after twenty minutes of being super upset over losing my fiancé, something shifted inside me. Everything was right, and a weight lifted, and I didn't feel bad at all because I'd never violated her in my heart. Despite the sour ending, it was my relationship with Tara that helped me come to a more correct realization about love.

I was doing a big activation for a cellphone company in Philadelphia. We had made a full-size bank vault, and as you walked up, you got your eyes scanned, and then the door to this full-size fake bank vault opens. I'm working the bank vault when this girl walks up. She's six feet tall, skinny, beautiful, and has the most gorgeous brown hair. And she's in three-inch heels.

I'm 5'11 so she's got four inches on me, and I'm looking up at her, thinking, *Wow, you're pretty, but I don't have a chance*, so I don't get my heart into it. I'm business-first when I'm at work, so I had that quick *oh wow!* moment and then shut it down, and I kept going. I show her what we do on the tablet, and she asks, "What backend are you using?"

My jaw drops. *What? Wait, wait, wait. What?*

"Are you running on this Node JS? Is this JavaScript?"

Immediately, I got sprung like Sir Mix-a-lot, metaphorically. That's what one singular question did for me, but I'm cool, and we go through the whole presentation. Then I forget all about her because this girl is way out of my league. Okay, not "totally cool," but I held it together. I'm just some nerd that builds stuff and owns a tech company.

When we do activations on our projects, we often tour. For example, business-to-business between top cell phone companies and the carriers means they go to different locations to have parties for the executives so everybody can mingle and meet and spend hundreds of thousands of dollars on interaction and automation. Tara is on the same circuit as me, so I ran into her on a circuit in Vegas.

They have booths that rain on the phones, and when you reach through, the rain has to stop so your hand stays dry, but the phone's wet, yet it still works. They seemed to come up with the craziest things for me to build, and I'd have to build them in no time. I'd more or less forego sleep for two weeks on end. We'd build a massive activation that's super complex, and then we'd have to tour while I couldn't see straight.

In Vegas, Tara's working as a model/product expert with two roles. Her beauty is used to get the executive perverts to say, "Show me more," but she also has to be intelligent enough to discuss the product. So we run into each other and have a "Hey, how are you?" moment, and then we each go about working the interactions.

She pulls me aside a little later and says, "You're a lot different from the rest of the executives here. One of the younger brand ambassadors said that you treated her like a human. Nobody else in your position does that."

"Well, she's a person," I say. "I don't feel like we're any different. She's got a job, I've got a job. We're done."

She smiles. "That's cool."

I run into her again at Fashion Week, and of course, she looks gorgeous. We're doing the Macy's Fashion Show in Union Square, and I say hello and blow her off, but I don't even realize I do that because I'm insanely working. I don't even remember seeing her there until she mentions it later.

A few weeks later, I run into her in Dallas, and she's just way too beautiful. She comes to me and asks, "Do you want to get together after the show?" and when I nod, she asks for my phone and types in her number, hands it back to me, and walks away after saying, "Text me later."

So I did.

The next day, we get together at a bar. We talk about how her father and mother had cancer, and she says she wants to create a social network for cancer patients. She wants tips and tricks on how to build the network. We get deeper and deeper into the conversation as I do the sexiest things you can imagine.

First, I smoke as many cigarettes as I can. She doesn't smoke; I come to find out.

Then I get drunk out of my mind. She doesn't drink; I come to find out.

And the coup de grâce is when I get trashed because the bartender gives us whiskey shots, and I'm shooting both hers and mine because she doesn't drink. Then I throw up all night. This is when that whole rock star thing crashes into reality.

The next day, I sleep behind a chair in the hotel while the activation for the new phone release is going on. I task my employees with stuff while I'm throwing up, hiding, or sleeping. I don't see Tara for a minute after that, and I'm pretty sure I blew that thing.

Understandably.

Then out of the blue, she texts me, and we start texting nonstop about everything. I'm mind blown. She's a southern belle from Tennessee. She's Christian. She's everything I want, as I want a sweet girl. And she's a virgin. I mean, who at thirty years of age is a virgin in our world?

One day, she says, "I will be in Seattle next week for work."

"Do you want me to meet you there?"

"Yes," she says. But her one precondition is, "If we do this, and I tell you to stop, you stop. We will sleep in the same bed, but if I say stop, you stop, and you be respectful."

So we meet in Seattle, and it's super awkward. I'm acting overconfident and cocky because I'm nervous. Our first kiss is the kind when you lean in and collide, and your noses run into each other, and it just sucks.

Tara brings me these cream cheese balls, explaining that they're some kind of southern treat. I'm super lactose intolerant, but I eat one anyway, and then I'm sick all night. We meet these people downstairs in the hotel who are visiting for a truffle convention. I tell her, "You're trouble—no, you're *truffle*." So her nickname is Truffles thereto forward.

By the end of the night, I guess she hates me, but she still wants to kiss me, and things happen, and I'm respectful. The next morning, we get up and check out the town. It's raining, so I give her my scarf and buy an umbrella for her. In the afternoon, I ask, "Do you want to be my girlfriend?"

"I do. I hated you yesterday, but I like you today, you're sweet." See, already the software thing was making itself known. But I wasn't paying attention; Eros was driving the boat.

Those two days in Seattle have marked the beginning of our relationship. Two weeks later she says, "You're a child, so meet me in St. Louis." I wonder who the hell wants to go to the Midwest for a date.

She says, "Just trust me."

St. Louis has this ten-story old shoe factory that's refashioned into a play place for adults. It's called City Museum, and everyone should go there at least once. Everyone. I walk in, and my first thought is, "I'm on a date with the hottest girl I've ever met, and I want to go jump on that rock over there and look like Spider-Man." For a few seconds, I wonder what to do until I run over and Spider-Man on the rock and then play all day while she sits there laughing and watching me be an idiot.

We spend that week getting close, and somehow in this, she decides to lose her virginity to me. I say, "No, I don't want that. We don't want that."

But she says, "Yes, we do."

So there's that.

She's living in Nashville, Tennessee, while I'm sleeping on a futon in my shop in Los Angeles in a nine-thousand-square-foot warehouse full of the newest tools in the world. I crash on the futon because I'm generally not super interested in paying rent. Since I'm there sixteen hours a day, it makes little sense to rent an apartment just to have a proper bed.

(This lifestyle is nothing new. While working at the top tech company in the world, I slept in a dirty garage for two years. I slept in a penthouse that was an office. For five years total, I didn't have a home. I was making six-plus figures, sometimes more, sleeping in random spots or my car.)

My goal with Tara is to see her at least once every two weeks in whichever city we can. We use all the airline miles we'd grabbed from the 160,000 miles I flew that year. We meet up in a new city, a new place, and experience all these new, exciting things. She moves to Dallas for work, but she hates it there, and since she's feeling hollow and empty, I keep flying out to see her.

We talk, but we never *talk*. Our software isn't aligned: it's destructive interference at its finest. We get into these weird fights, one of them being I have a big job to do over the

Thanksgiving vacation, but I spend five days with her family anyway. When I tell her I have to leave a day early, she freaks out. "You don't want to spend time with me! You don't spend enough time with my family!"

I say, "Truffles, you don't understand. I see my family about once every three years, and I try to get out of there as fast as I can. I just spent more time with your family than I have with mine in years. You got a big win there."

"Well, it's not enough," she says.

I'm thinking about the possibility of our software being misaligned. Instead of thinking that I'm detached from family and that family is important to her, I'm thinking about the fight. If the family is not important to me, we will always have the fight when I want to be with family for two days instead of six.

Now I would look at the fight from the outside. Instead of being in the fight, I'd watch it as an observer and explore why it's happening. My way's not bad and her way's not bad if we're equally happy or equally unhappy. It's just a matter of avoiding these fights, but I don't look at it the right way at this time. I look at it as, "I'm right. Stop messing with my life."

It makes more sense to ask questions and listen to the answers instead of dreaming about a circuit I will build or planning how to put two pieces of metal together in one half of my brain while the other half is mumbling answers to Tara.

That's a big problem for me and you, this dichotic brain. Maybe you're not thinking about circuits, gears, and software.

You might think about Kanye and Kim or that new Biebs song that's just rad when you should shut off the rest of your brain and ask, "Why are we in this fight?" Anytime you have something come up, ask why. Practice that kind of analysis instead of thinking you're just flat-out right.

The fights with Tara multiply and pile up. I've been talking about the company that I own with partners in Nicaragua for a year, and I tell her we're going to Nicaragua to see them. We'll stay at the hotel, but I have a couple of meetings I need to attend. But she doesn't hear any of that either. As soon as she gets on the plane, I say, "I'm going to meet with Brad when I land."

She's mad during the whole flight. And when we land, she's still mad. She says, "You didn't tell me this was a work trip."

"It's not a work trip. I just have a couple of hours where I need to meet with my partners."

She's just crappy the whole time we are there. There's this one moment in my head where I think, *I'm in fucking Nicaragua. I'm going to have fun.* I look over at her and say, "If you won't have fun, that's fine. But I'm going to have fun."

I get invited to their super-exclusive ayahuasca ceremony where you trip balls in the jungle for eight hours, and I want to do this. She says, "If you go, I won't go with you, and I will leave you."

That was another key moment when I should have looked at our exchange rather than wondering, *Why are you doing this to me?* I thought I could change her mind, but I should have realized this was a template problem.

The first time we met, I told her I smoked weed, so it wasn't like I was hiding it. I don't smoke anymore, but at the time, I did. She hates that I smoke weed and says she shouldn't have to change for me; instead, I should just stop (or change for her). She's intolerant. I never ask her to like it, but I should see that this intolerance is something that's a principle and important to her. Instead, I say, "You're just not open-minded."

You can't label the person as a thing; you should look at the situation instead. Understand that everybody is right in their feelings. If you're not hurting somebody, you can't say that their feelings are wrong. But when you get in that moment, you think, *Oh, she's a bitch. He's a dick.*

That's not the answer. They feel different, and maybe they're more reactive than you, but you might harbor things. So look at what's important to them and look at what's important to you and ask if the two can line up. Can you negotiate to a middle ground, or are you always going to conflict?"

My love for Tara is the most mature love I've had, but it's also immature that I don't take the time to understand her software. The truth is that we are different. We have different experiences. We have different understandings. Our trip to Nicaragua throws a spotlight on where we diverge, and it's the beginning of the final downfall.

When our split finally happens, she throws a lot of insults at me; she says a lot of ugly things. She destroys me. I've just taken a big payout from a company, and she says, "You're leaving me because you have money now, and you'll go with your Nicaraguan surfing girls." I'm staying in Nicaragua when we split, so I'm surrounded by beautiful surfer women, yet I've been all in with my fiancé. I don't see the other women as anything but humans. They aren't objects to me, and I'm not checking them out. I'm not trying to hook up or even remotely desire them.

Tara has left me twice before, and while she's yelling at me this last time, I say, "I think we're headed in separate directions."

She's been telling me where we're moving. I'm saying that where we move should be a joint decision. She says it's not and that we're moving to Tennessee. I ask if we can talk about it and figure out what's best for both of us, but she insists, "No, we're moving to Tennessee."

I'm not okay with this.

After thirty minutes of feeling destroyed by her insults, I have this moment. You know how in cartoons where a light bulb pops up over someone's head? Well, mine pops up, and I know that our software is misaligned—the way Tara sees things differs from my reality, and there's no fixing this.

I have done none of the things she blames on me. I felt none of those things she accuses me of. I never cheated on her in my heart. Suddenly, I feel this weight lift from me as I download this intense new understanding.

If this is how she sees things and this is how she feels, then we would have been screwed for the rest of our lives if we stay together. I'm sad that our relationship ends, but I know I dodged a bullet, and it's my fault for not listening sooner.

Love is about listening to the other person and considering their perspective. The sooner you can do that, the sooner you can see if your software aligns—and the less time you will waste. Love is the balancing act between being single, which is enjoyable, and being with someone, which can waste time or be boring. We expect things that are black and white to be bad, but they rarely are. There is some balance between the two, and it comes down to figuring out that person's software as quickly as you can.

There's no need to tell someone your darkest secrets on the first day you meet. But within the first couple of months, you shouldn't have anything you're hiding from them, or you're wasting time. Being with someone just to be with someone, or because society tells you should, means you're wasting time and money. If you want to act because someone says, "Oh my God, you're thirty years old, and you're not married? That's weird," then you better run.

Take the time to learn the person. Be brave enough to split it off early. That sounds like a cold thing, but you have to win fast or fail fast in business—the same applies to love. Maybe you dive in too deep while controlling your heart, but you need to solve quickly whether it will work or it's a colossal waste of time for both of you. I would never say that two months is a waste of time, but at three months, you always know. But then some people spend ten years complaining about it anyway.

On a buddy's wedding night, his bride said, "I'm not taking your name. We won't be married long enough for that to matter."

I asked, "Why the hell did you get married then? Just end it. You're afraid to be alone? You'll be fine. You won't die."

The balancing act is going in with logic and checking that software alignment. That's how you achieve balance. Being with someone isn't a waste of time, but being with the wrong person wastes time—yours and theirs. There should be no fear of being alone, and there should be no fear of exposing yourself. If that person leaves, then they left, and that's that. It has to be right for both people.

What are the options for ethical, casual relationships when you crave physical intimacy but find yourself impatient with the social time investment? Rub one out. That's it. The name of my book shows that I did my dalliances, and I can guarantee you there is not a single one-night stand that won't mess with you. Rub it out. There is no other ethical way.

The biggest tactic for developing relationships is to bring them into your world.

My love is for building, and I'm not as good at building when I watch TV with my girlfriend because I'm not getting better at my skill. What I love about Annie is that we don't have to watch TV. She'll come into the garage and ask, "How do I solder this? How do I wire that up? How do I use the angle grinder? Can I use that mill?"

It's not that she enjoys those things, but that she's getting into my world. Love can make you boring when you're compromising the middle ground and watching TV. I hate going to the park, and that's okay because she goes alone with her kid if I choose not to go. If I were to always agree to join, I wouldn't be myself. But if I were to never acquiesce, that would make me a dick.

Whatever your world is, be honest with whom you bring in. If you want that relationship to survive, and you don't want to be bored, then figure out how to be excited together. And it doesn't have to be building crap in the garage. You can be an awesome snowboarder who goes on the bunny hill with your partner so you can do it together. Find things to do together.

Experiencing a flow state with a loved one.

Maybe you do yoga together side-by-side in a flow state. But even then, a flow state is your personal thing. When my girlfriend is clipping wires in her flow state and getting things prepped for me and I'm soldering things together and building the small units, we're both in a flow state. We're not talking. We're both going, and when we speak, it's something like, "You're behind."

"Oh, here's two more."

"Thanks."

You can have that personal state, but you can't be talking about emotions. You can't be arguing—be in it together. A flow is a personal thing, but you can do it in the community. Hence, full rooms of people doing yoga together.

The relationship I'm currently in is the first time I've ever had a flow with another human being, and I'm enjoying it. But first, I had to let her into my world. She hasn't been soldering crap for twenty years like I have, and she had to want to do it alongside me. If she wants to learn how to write code, I could show her how because that's fun. That's what I like to do, and I should want to do the things I want to do with my partner. But it was always my fault I didn't have this kind of flow before, and I have no one to blame but myself.

If the whole time I'm with her, I'm saying, "I want to get in my flow state instead," then that doesn't work. Or maybe I'd take a lesser flow state for a while because she's in the house watching TV and I'm thinking, *I can't get into the flow because now I feel bad she's inside, and now she'll be mad at me.*

If you want a mature relationship, then bring them into every facet of your life. They might not want to be in all of them, but let them try them all, and you try all of theirs. Anything you expect of them, you should expect of yourself for them. I get it now, but it took me thirty-five years to get here.

Boredom

Love makes you boring and dull.

Be careful not to lose yourself in a relationship. Just as with anything else, the kids shouldn't own you, the dog shouldn't own you, and the relationship shouldn't own you. It should build you up and make you better or more of what you are. And if it's not? You will become boring. You will become useless. You will become dull.

You'll come home from work every day and ask, "When's dinner?" You'll go into work Monday morning, and when everybody is talking about what they did over the weekend, instead of being the one who says, "I woke up in my car in the casino parking lot with an extra $300 and a hangover," you'll be the one who says, "I cut the lawn."

Well, you let yourself become boring.

Don't lose yourself, but also make sure that your interests line up or can overlap to where you can do things you love together. Otherwise, it's a waste. It's that software needing to line up again. It may turn out that she likes the crap you do. Find that middle ground where you can do what you love to do and not impact the relationship. Otherwise, you will become boring, dull, and bitter.

Boredom—or rather, the avoidance of that state— is the force that drives me.

Kids today get bored much more quickly than most of my generation did. If they go ten minutes without their iPad, they'd lose their minds because they need input all the time. I get it because I'm the same way. I get bored in a relationship. I get bored doing a hobby. Sometimes I get bored of being bored. I had to learn that boredom happens, and it's my responsibility to find positive ways to deal with it.

When I was thirteen, my grandmother asked me, "What does it feel like to be a genius?" And without thinking or hesitating, I looked at her and said, "Boring."

Boredom is that numbed-out dead time when you're in a room surrounded by activity, yet nothing seems to register. Have you ever been in the desert sun? You'll hear that deafening silence. You can literally see boredom in those old Western movies where the sun's blazing hot, and the heat is coming up from the desert floor, and all you hear is that low, buzzing noise.

That desert feeling is the only thing I can equate to what it feels like to wait forty-five minutes before a conference call, and I don't have a good block of time to invest in something. This is the world I get stuck in, and it draws out for days and days. If I don't have a four-hour block to get into the flow, then I hit a brick wall and lose my track.

Boredom has always been my greatest fear. I'd much rather be tortured or have a screaming headache than be bored. Probably the reason my relationships have fallen apart is that I fear having two kids and imagining that I have to take the kids to soccer practice in forty-five minutes, then I won't be able to get into the flow, and the rest of my day will be boring.

Boredom is a searing pain, the worst I can imagine. Everything I do is to avoid boredom and get into that flow state, that anti-boredom. If I'm half into something, it's torture. I can write the software, but it will take twenty times as long. If I have an hour, I won't get anything done because I know it'll take twenty times as long, so I may as well wait for a two to four-hour block and nail it to the wall.

In the meantime, there's boredom.

But boredom isn't necessarily a bad thing. It can push us to do our best things whether that's rocking code, racing cars, skateboarding, or equally fun and stupid ideas. Used properly, boredom can be our greatest driver for good or, in an unfortunate moment, evil.

What are the best responses to boredom?

Frivolity isn't a normal state for most. Say, you want to be a rock star or a race car driver. You get bricked if you don't have a four-hour block of time to bang on the drums or build something. But engaging in something frivolous can easily take you into a creative direction.

To stave off the boredom blues, get silly. If you're a rock star, write a stupid song, which doesn't have to be your masterpiece. Design something hillbilly for fun. For me, it's popping something stupid off on the laser cutter. Make a snowflake, and send it to somebody. Put some bad words on a piece of Lexan, and laugh when it's lit up and hanging on your wall. Have a few beers with your buddy, and see which pieces in the garage you can turn into a guitar amp.

We spend so much time focusing on that serious end goal that we forget that letting loose and having some fun can help you reach that goal. Even if you're just riding a shopping cart down a set of stairs, at least you're learning how to fall.

Einstein said, "Imagination is more important than knowledge. For knowledge is limited to all we now know and understand, while imagination embraces the entire world, and all there ever will be to know and understand."

What kinds of building blocks are nearby? All things around you are an assemblage of pieces, which means it's okay to take apart the VCR, pull the motors out, and build some Rube Goldberg machine—or build nothing and mess it all up. Who cares? There are lots of VCRs in the world.

Children play all day, and that's what they do right. How often do you see a child bored? Only when you stick them in a place where they're not allowed to break stuff or stab it together. As adults, we lose our imagination. We build toy stores for children with big things to play in, but how many such things do we have for adults? We've got bars and race cars, of course, but everything has a high point of entry.

When was the last time you zipped down a slide or straddled the monkey bars? Why not retain that imagination that there's lava or a dragon over there you must avoid? Once you lose your imagination, all that's left are drugs, gossip, and TV. Instead, look at something through a child's eyes and remember to play. When I look at a 3D printer, all I see are motors, bars, a plastic case, and a circuit board. And that's what kids see because they don't know what the big thing is, but they know how to take that piece and that piece and that piece and put them together, and bam—they've got a cabin or a castle!

A case of boredom can lead to awesomeness.

I remember drinking my face off in my college dorm room, which happened often. Sometimes stupidity ensued. We're all bored at college, so we make up a thing called sack ball, which is where you throw a tennis ball down the hallway and hit each other in the sack. This was a great game we often play while drinking. Or we box in the hallway. It turns out I'm a terrible boxer; I get knocked out every time.

One day, this shirtless dude, Ralph—a big farmer guy who weighed about 250 pounds—walks up to me and says, "Ah, you're drunk again."

That was neither here nor there. "Who are you?"

"I'm Ralph. You want to race cars?"

"Sure, I want to race cars."

"Cool," he says. "We started this club, and that's what we're going to do."

I'm thinking this club is a formal, registered student organization. Nope. This is where one professor gives his garage and a bunch of crappy cars to his students. Awesome! So we get drunk and race cars, which is loads of fun for a bunch of dirty, swearing, nasty, stinky college guys.

Pure frivolity, right?

Yet we're in the first crew to race the infield of the Milwaukee Mile when it reopened. Plus, we join the SCCA (Sports Car Club of America) and the MCSCC (Midwestern Council Sports Car Club). We're still doing the things we did before like drinking, carousing, and smoking, but we also learn how things work mechanically and how to break things and put them back together again.

We buy a 1989 Honda Civic for a hundred bucks, take all the seats out, bang the frame straight because it was in a rollover accident, put it all back together, and off-road it against a 1984 diesel Rabbit. We camp in the middle of the racetrack in the dark. We "crash-truck," which is where you get up at 7:00 a.m., pull all the crashed cars off the racetrack, and then we race for free on the closed days at the track.

Plus, the track was private property, so drunk driving a 1982 Mazda RX-7 was totally legal, and we would do up to 110 or 120—just drunk out of our minds. Since there was only one wall on the whole racetrack, we'd spin out and slide across the grass. It was an absolutely amazing time.

Another plus to racing was taking girls out on the racetrack because if you took a girl on the racetrack, you had a date after that. I guarantee you it worked every time. You didn't even have to be a good driver (I certainly wasn't). The best I ever did was take second place, but I got a lot of dates out of that track.

I remember one particular time when I took a girl who was significantly out of my league out on the track. On this day, I pushed the car a bit too hard and blew a linkage, causing the car to spin across the track's infield at high speed. We spun six or seven times, finally resting dead center of the track, in the grass with me stuck in "full-on grin" mode. She looked at me with wild eyes, then proceeded to pull her top down and show me her breasts. To this day, I don't have any clue as to why.

My advice is to keep your eyes open when you're bored and when somebody asks you a crazy question. Often the best things that ever happened to me have come out of somebody asking me a dumb question and me giving the dumbest answer possible.

Dumb question asker: "Hey, man, you wanna join me to do this thing?"

Me: "Huh? Sure. Fuck it. I got nothing else going on."

Boredom goes awry.

Life is about contrast, so all my stories can't have a happy ending. That'd be like all five-star dinners where life is always perfect, and you never learn you don't like ramen noodles. With that in mind, there are a few ways boredom led me to a more destructive or unproductive path.

When I was nineteen years old, I bought a Toyota Supra on eBay and thought, *Screw it, I'll go pick it up.* I look at a waitress next to me at this restaurant and ask, "Do you want to go to Virginia Beach with me?"

She nods in agreement.

The next day, we hop on a train to Virginia Beach. The whole three days we're both super awkward, and when I want to hook up, she says, "Nah, I got a boyfriend." When she wants to hook up, I say, "No, I have a girlfriend." It's a weird tap dance, and nothing ever happens.

We hit Virginia Beach, and I procure this great beachside hotel on the fifth floor with a balcony—complete with an epic view of a 7-11 convenience store. Beachside was expensive, just saying. We try to get beer, and after having forty dollars stolen by people we ask to buy it for us, we get smart and say we'll only give them the money after having the beer in our hands. That works, and we drink our faces off on this balcony, gazing at the partially lit neon of the beachside 7-11 store.

This dude comes out on the balcony next to us and asks if he can have a beer. I hand him a cold one, and we talk. Turns out he's a pimp, and he says, "Come on over here and party with me." So I climb over the precarious fifth-story balcony gap to his room as the waitress, Jill, says, "You know, there's a door. We could just go around." But by that time, I was already on his balcony.

We hang out in the room together, and when we hear a knock, the pimp says, "One of my girls coming back." Now I've never seen a hooker in my life. Christian parents raised me, and I'm still a somewhat well-to-do whitebread kid at that point. I don't know what to expect.

She walks in, and she looks precisely as I would have imagined a real hooker to look, complete with stretch marks on the places squeezed out of her undersized strappings of what I supposed were clothes. I mean, she's rough; definitely, some bad times have happened to this woman. She sits next to me. "Hundred bucks, and I'll give you a good time."

Apparently, I respond, "If you pay *me* $10,000, I still won't do it." This is unfortunate, but I was not so nice as a kid. I'm probably still not nice.

Anyway, I guess—and I don't remember this—but Jill told me that they brought out some crack and asked if I wanted to try it.

"Yes," I say. *Oh, the boredom strikes back.*

"We won't give you the pipe. We're gonna have to shotgun."

"I'm not putting my lips where somebody else's have been," I say. "We're gonna do this through a toilet paper tube."

So apparently that happened.

I wake up the next morning with the most awful drip down my nose, feeling more like death than I've ever felt. I have to drive sixteen hours home in a Toyota Supra that's missing a headlight and has a turbo issue, so it won't go above fifty-five miles an hour.

I see a body with a sheet over it on a road in the Maryland mountains on the way back. *That could be me right now,* I think, but it wasn't, luckily. But that weekend was one of those times where afterward I realized that my actions were just plain stupid.

Was that enough to keep me from going off the rails again?

Reasonably bored in big boy office life.

I found myself bored with life. I was living the type of life after being hired by the top electronic devices company in the world, the kind of company that kids like me drool over. Yet I was bored; I wasn't challenged. I was good at my job—I just wasn't good at what to do with myself after work. I was lonely, as well. I worked too much and didn't have enough people in my life I could trust.

Dangerous combination.

Love isn't something that falls in naturally because I love work so much. I'm married to it, in fact. And so I'm bored, on a night off, swiping through Tinder for a distraction. Tinder is fun because I'm in control. I'm powerful, but I'm the decider (or so I think). I flip through the images, and I see this tall girl that's prettier than any of the others.

I swipe right.

So does she.

Her profile doesn't say what she does for work, but okay, cool. I'm bored. Her choice of career doesn't matter. I suggest we meet at this classy bar across the street from my house. I'm not saying that I'm lazy; I'm saying that it doesn't seem like a good idea to do anything but walk half a block for a Tinder date.

I get in my three-piece suit and head across the street to the appropriately named Noir Lounge and sit at the bar. She shows up, and my first thought is that she's a lot taller than I thought. My second thought is that she's pretty.

Then she laughs, and my third thought is that she has a horrifying laugh.

This laugh is beyond horrifying, as this woman is not cultured at all. Easily, she makes me look classy, which is tough to do unless I'm trying. But we're still laughing and joking. When she goes to the bathroom, another girl at the bar says to me, "Picked yourself a winner there, huh?"

"I guess. I don't know," I say, because the booze is kicking in, and although we're not quite at *all is well,* we're getting closer.

I know the bartender, so she feeds me free drinks all night until I'm trashed. Maybe I do it on purpose, you know, to lubricate the passing of time. I also dated the bartender at one point… oops.

When the Noir Lounge closes, we head across the street to another bar. In the next frame, we're making out. It becomes some bad movie when this guy randomly pulls our stools out from under us as he walks by. Perhaps, he tires of hearing that horrifying laugh.

We fall on the ground and knock heads. I pull her necklace off as I fall, and it shatters into a million pieces across the floor. Now we're kludging around and trying our drunken best to pick up all these little blurry pieces of the necklace.

"Let's find a place with a pool! Let's get a hotel," she suggests.

"Yeah, let's get a hotel with a pool." I agree because it seems like a great idea. The last thing either of us needs is a pool, but we forget about that, which is probably a fortunate thing. We go to a hotel and stay up all night doing, you know, naughty stuff. Her choice of a career becomes obvious—the girl can move around a pole, that's for sure.

I wake up at about six thirty on what I think is the next morning and realize it's not Saturday—it's Monday. I've been doing the girl and coke for three days straight because I was bored out of my mind and thought a good distraction would be to swipe right.

Nausea kicks in, and it's crawling up my throat. I'm out of cocaine, and I have to get home, but we're at breakfast, and I'm trying not to throw up. I want more cocaine to make it through the day because I feel crispy and dead inside. I want to get away from this girl because suddenly I feel the shame I should have felt before, but I was lonely and drinking. Now all I see is the mess. Her hair. My face in the mirror.

Somebody has smashed the window of my car, so I drive to work in my BMW 328i with a broken window. I'm utterly disheveled—long hair flying from the wind rushing in through the broken window. My tie is hanging to the left. A couple of buttons popped off my suit, and I'm missing a cuff link on that poor white Thomas Pink shirt. Yet I'm smoking a cigarette out the window while driving to work at a tech giant with a smirk on my face.

I fucking made it.

This is the most rock star I will ever be as an engineer, I just know it. I stayed up having sex with a stripper all night. Hell, for three nights. You can use your imagination to fill in the blanks. Normally, I'm more graphic, but I'm trying to be classy.

That moment when the sun comes out and the headache comes in, I've slid home into a Quentin Tarantino movie— disgusting, horrible, sweaty, slimy, sticky, gross. Sometimes there just aren't enough adjectives. Luckily, I had an office with frosted windows, so I locked the door and pretended like I was busy until I face planted on the keyboard. You know when you wake up and the home row is molded on your forehead? That was me.

jakfdssdfdsfdsfsdfdsfsdfdsfdsfdsfsd…

The next day, I think I'm okay. I'm still feeling tired, but I go to the Silicon Design Review meeting where we're architecting a chip, which is very complex work. You have to know how the software works. You have to know how silicon works. You have to understand these gates and transistors. We're trying to figure out how to put these matrices into ROM (read-only memory, always static, stable, the same).

Suddenly, my eyes start ripping around in random directions. *Holy shit.* My heart's missing every third beat. I have to get water; I must be dehydrated. But then I'm on a stretcher, and they're racing me to the health center on campus. They put me on an EKG, and one valve of my heart isn't doing what it's supposed to. The electrical signal's missing.

They rush me to the hospital and put in an IV, and within a few hours, everything's fine, and nobody can figure out what happened to me. I don't tell anybody that I did a stripper and three days' worth of cocaine. I remained mum about that and only admitted to smoking some weed here and there. For weeks on end, I go to cardiologist appointments. They scratch their heads and say, "But your heart is strong." I try to keep up the facade there might be something wrong with my heart, but I know that my heart is fine.

But there's something wrong with my head because I keep doing these things.

Channeling boredom.

I've always had a multitude of projects going, such as a robot, woodworking, art, a car, and a motorcycle project. I always have probably five to ten projects open that I may never finish. But the reason being is if I am bored, I can think about what excites me and go play with it. What I find is that if I tinker with something for five minutes, it will grab me, and suddenly, I'm back in that positive place and not sitting there with that heart-wrenching pain stuck against a wall of boredom.

You may not want to pick up a project when you're bored and want to sit there and complain, but you know you have to do something. I don't care what it is. Pick up crap from the floor. Polish some silverware. Wash the windows. Get into a groove, and next thing you know, you're in a flow state again.

All you want to do when you're bored is to stay bored. Nothing is exciting. But you have to learn how to manipulate your environment. You have things that will stimulate you again to create that situation for yourself to help your behavior.

Dealing with boredom on the job.

You may have to endure this kind of boredom until you make it to your goals. The thing I've always found to be helpful is to do ancillary tasks. Do your work, but find a way to put something else in there that trips your trigger. An example of this would be at a tech company when I was sick of doing this same semiconductor crap over and over: I learned how to do web servers and linked that into the testing of the semiconductors.

I learned to do login and authentication parallel to my normal work, and it boosted my interest all around. When I was working on gaming headphones, I learned how to code Windows and Mac programs that would control the headphones. My job was the silicon, but what I was interested in was graphics and how to make an eloquent, beautiful user interface.

What came of making my own user interface was that I got even more accolades because they said, "Not only did he do his job, he also handed us a better user interface to go with us than the one we had." The trick is to get excited and feel driven and then get excited about your day job to make it link into this other piece you're excited about. It's better to ask for forgiveness instead of permission, and when you blow the boss's mind, they're stoked. Sometimes they'll feel jealous and ruin your life, but hey, at least you had fun.

Don't miss your deadlines to add fun to your job. For example, some things I worked on at home at night. If you're behind on your work, and you're doing side gigs, that's a problem. That's called immaturity, and you might get fired. But if you're hitting your deadlines, and deadlines are generally easy, then you're cool.

Every job seems structured for the people who don't want to be there, I've found. Schedules are in place to keep people there because they're not in the zone. When you're in the zone, your job takes about an hour a day. If you're excited about that thing you're doing and if something can get you excited about your core job, now everything happens, and you probably skipped lunch because you were stoked and not bored that day.

Having an enemy takes away boredom.

Start competing with the surrounding people. Instead of thinking, *That guy over there sucks at circuit boards, and I'm a software guy*, why not get into a circuit board and fix it? Start a friendly competition and then open up your software and say, "Hey, I'm not being a dick. You can fix my software." And maybe it doesn't even need to be a friendly war. Some of my competitions might not have been friendly, but they drove both parties to excel.

It can be a friendly enemy, a buddy of mine, or a straight-up enemy, but that competition removes boredom because now you've got something to fight for. Humans were born to fight, yet we are polite and passive-aggressive. I think I've hit one person in my life in seventh grade, and then I had a panic attack, and I think he had the same.

I'm not a good fighter, but it's in our nature to fight however we can. And fighting with our wits is a way to sharpen all of us. Puppies play to learn the rules and to get better at things; we should all play like puppies.

Boredom is not an excuse for burning bridges, yet I've done it.

I've driven myself insane and left a job when I didn't find a positive way to exit. That's not good; it always has ramifications. I'm good at arguing, so I felt like I "won." But I'm not sure I won because of the weight I had to carry after I left. Even if it feels like you win in those situations, you never win when you let your emotions prevent you from respecting somebody else's feelings, job, or time.

Recently, I reached out to a bunch of people I had burned and apologized because I couldn't carry that feeling around anymore. I said, "I was bored, so I was a jerk to you and said some mean things and tore you apart and still got my money." I had to clear that with them.

The apologies worked, and now we're on great terms, and the next time I'm in LA, we'll get together for drinks. But I had to drop all hubris and offer no excuses. I acted like a dick, and I had to apologize. It was unfair of me to say such things because I thought they were idiots. I still do. But just because they're not good at what they do doesn't make them less human.

When we hurt people, we might think we take power out of it, but we carry bitter, evil, nasty resentment, and it drags us down. Now I feel like a weight has been lifted. I don't harbor resentment toward those people who once angered me. They're good dudes, and I'm stoked to grab a drink with them one day. We had a lot of good times too.

Strife

We need boredom to drive us into strife.

I had this idea to purchase a shipping container, put it on a hill, and live in it; I was all in for the concept. However, the concept differed substantially from reality. I was suffering so hard; I was freezing, as I had to sleep in a tent until I could get the rat poison out of the container. That wasn't easy either, replacing the floor in the middle of nowhere with only hand tools and manual labor.

Details, details.

I'll be the first to tell you: sleeping in a tent during a desert winter sucks. But the day I finally got electricity was the best day of my life. The moment I got firewood was also the best day of my life. And the moment I got a propane heater was also the best day of my life.

See the pattern?

I kept having these best days of my life because a medium life makes everything medium: there's no contrast. But a bad life is the real gift because it makes everything amazing in comparison. When you're poor, it's awesome, and when you get rich, it sucks. That's how I know we need boredom to lead into strife.

I was always different from the other kids. To me, they epitomized that old phrase "happy-go-lucky," and that was never me; I was too busy trying to fight the boredom. I didn't feel connections with the other kids, and I've never been good at the whole friend thing. However, I was always very empathetic. If somebody got hurt, even on TV, it would upset me inside. Although I never felt strong connections *to* other people, I always feel *for* other people, which is probably why I'm a terrible CEO.

When I was younger, attempting to live the typical dream created an internal conflict for me. I wanted to make my parents proud: I wanted to be Bill Gates—the proper, upstanding nerd, not a fucking hippie—and that dude seems so well-adjusted. There was pride in that goal, and I looked forward to achieving it.

Everybody else wanted to be Steve Jobs. They thought they related to him and wanted to see themselves as the *Jobs alpha* in any situation. But I understood why Jobs was an asshole: he saw everything light-years before everyone else. The people around him annoyed him, and he had to grind his teeth and wait for them to catch up.

When I was fourteen years old, I did some database work for my dad because that's what I thought I wanted. I wanted that office. I wanted that cubicle. I wanted to wear the suit, but I also wanted to be a rock star and an artist. The problem was that I could be anything I wanted to be because almost everything

I touched was easy to do for a living. Maybe I wasn't going to be the best at whatever, but no doors seemed closed.

Three bunny hops right out of school, I took a job that most people retire in. Yet the pieces of myself I was giving up didn't seem to balance out once I started working on supercars as a system architect a couple of decades sooner than I should have. Timing is everything, as they say.

What's the point of this? I wondered. Suddenly, there was nothing left to chase except the CEO position, and I "couldn't have that with my earrings," or so I've been told. It was the same pattern as always: once I got the thing I wanted— whether it was the girl, the job, or anything else—I was conflicted and bored.

Sometimes a thing we want doesn't turn out to be what we want. You don't know what you don't know, so it's stupid to want something you don't really understand. I wanted to work in an office, but the idea didn't equate with the reality of living that dream. Just like living in that shipping container in the desert didn't jive with how I imagined the experience would be.

My search for a panacea drove me. I jumped in and out of career hot water. I worked for a semiconductor company where I worked on autonomous vehicles, teaching cars to drive themselves. I walked in one morning and saw all the clues, and so I asked them, "Are you laying me off?"

I was stoked when they told me I was being laid off, which sounds like a weird thing. I had no money, but I took my severance and started a company building and modifying motorcycles. Miss America even did a photoshoot with one of our bikes. Due to the low budget, I took the photos for it, as I was a photography student in my younger years.

Shortly thereafter, after the struggle, I had an opportunity to work in engineering on parts for supercars. That was the dream, the pinnacle, everything I ever wanted. Or so I thought.

That's the thing with boredom.

Bored on a Thursday.

I had nothing of importance to do on this random Thursday afternoon working for an Italian car company.

Cue boredom.

I'm sitting in my cubicle, bored out of my mind, coding for a six-figure car. I'm so sick of supercars I could shoot myself in the face. I have gotten nothing done for the past two hours when one of my buddies, Brandon, walks into the cubicle and asks, "What are you up to?"

"I was cruising the web. Did you know you can go on a cruise for three hundred bucks?"

"You can?"

"I've never been on a cruise. Have you?"

"Nah, I haven't. You want to go?"

So we press purchase on the tickets, and then we realize, *Oh crap, we have to tell our boss.*

My buddy is designing the circuit boards for the cars' gauge clusters, and I'm doing most of the firmware. There's no other team doing what we do, so the whole schedule slips by ten days if we do this. Now our boss was an Italian guy with a shaved head who always wore an expensive suit. Since I was a nice-suit man at the time, too, we got along famously. I respected the guy as he was super smart and very classy.

Except for that one day when he had walked into my office, looked at me, and said, "Hi."

He never did that, so I looked up and waited. "Hi."

He stood there for a second and then walked away. It confused me until it hit me: terrifying fart smell, *End of Days* style. The most proper man I'd ever met had crop dusted me.

Yet on this day we walk into his office and say, "Sorry, Agostino, we booked a cruise, and we need to go. We'll be back in a couple weeks."

He looks up from his desk. "You need to do what?"

"Well, to get to Florida in time, we have to leave in a couple of hours. So we're taking off."

He looks confused but says, "Okay."

Brandon and I pack everything up and cram into his small cab truck for a nineteen-hour drive from Detroit to Tampa. It was terrible. No sleep at all. Swallowing our knees while dreaming of a bench seat that reclines. We're exhausted when we get there, so we grab a hotel.

Brandon wants to meet up with a girl, but he has terrible luck with girls…because he's creepy. I love the guy, but he was super creepy back then. These days, he's probably less creepy than I on an average day. I'm exhausted, so we get into a big fight before boarding the cruise ship. Like I said, I'm not good at the whole friend thing. And because we're exhausted out of our minds, we immediately start drinking our faces off as soon as our feet hit the wooden deck of the ship. Profusely drinking.

I decide it's time to get in the three-piece and hit up the casino—because who doesn't love the casino? And blackjack is fun. So I put on my cuff links, $200 shirt, and $2,000 suit, which was a waste of money. But that's what I spent my first paycheck on because I'm a genius, obviously.

(I'm a complete idiot.)

I play blackjack, and the woman next to me is way too good-looking for me to even talk to. I'm a little nervous, but I'm in a suit, and I'm a little drunk, so let's do this. We chat, and I'm eyeing her and thinking she's fifteen or twenty years older than me. I later learn that she's eighteen years older, which meant she graduated high school the year I was born. It doesn't matter; we keep chatting. Whatever. I win some money or lose some money, but I'm pretty sure I lost, which isn't the point of the story. We go about our ways for that evening.

The next day, Brandon and I go to the beach. We buy some weed from a guy, but we're too scared to smoke it because the dealer told us, "Be careful and don't get caught, or you'll go to jail here for twenty years." We're scared out of our minds because we're young, so we don't know what to do once we buy it. Brandon suggests we eat it.

I've smoked a good amount of weed in my life, but I've never eaten weed straight up. But we do this anyway because it seems like the best idea, and we don't have enough money to get drunk. Totally forgot cash on the boat. We fall asleep on the beach, and when we wake up, we see this girl glide out of the water. She's beautiful; a '90s perfect 10 in a bikini. I swear she walks by in slow motion. Cue Phoebe Cates in *Fast Times at Ridgemont High*.

Of course, we're dropping our knockoff Ray-Bans down our noses and awkwardly staring because we're young guys, and you don't stare directly at the sun. Then she stops and smiles. "Hey, you."

Wait, what? Me?

It was the girl from the blackjack table the night before. She sits down next to me on my towel. Brandon is slack-jawed; I mean, he's not even talking at all. Maybe it's the weed, but probably not. But he wasn't at the casino, so he didn't know with whom I had spoken. She hangs out with us, and we have a great time.

The next day, we get together for Cirque du Soleil. She says that she's one of the original Hooter's models from the first year. I'm mind blown. I'm a kid from Detroit, and I've met no one famous before. Although a Hooter's model is D list, in Detroit, we don't even have that; we only have cars. On the last night of the cruise, I finally kiss her, and we end up dating for a time.

Because of one of those boredom moments, I end up dating one of the original Hooter's models for six months. And I get to meet Hulk Hogan with her.

Well, let me back up.

I didn't formally meet him. I was peeing in the bathroom of his restaurant when he walks in, looks at me, and says, "Bet you didn't know this was here, brother," and he enters a secret luxury bathroom.

Yes, that's right: I meet Hulk Hogan while holding my dick.

New chapters, more strife.

When we get back from the cruise, I give my two weeks' notice that very day and realize I have all these vacation days. I work one day after that and get paid for four weeks because it was over the Christmas holiday. Then I'm offered a small contract after I leave automotive life. So I take the contract, and about two and a half months into it, I have this big moral problem. Everybody there is a hillbilly; they're all C-plus engineers while pretending to be A-plus. I go through this Boeing training where nobody seems to know what the fuck they're doing.

If we build this thing we're supposed to build, we're literally going to kill people. There's no doubt about it. If there's no oxygen on this thing, it will take thirty seconds for the nitrogen in the air to saturate the bloodstream and kill people. And there will be no resuscitation.

These engineers are subpar, Midwest normal. I'm thinking maybe, just maybe, something akin to Apple engineers should do this kind of job, not these standard people. On the day I realize the seriousness of the situation, I tell the boss, "If we go to court, I can't back you up. I'll have to say that you guys were doing it wrong."

He loses it. "Get the fuck out of here."

"I'm sorry, this is just the way it is. I can work on your non-safety pieces as long as I don't have visibility into the safety, but I won't touch that kind of liability." This is a huge contract. I'm making ninety grand in three months at my young age. I understand that a salary like this is world-changing—yet I'll kill somebody if I take this money and do this job.

This gig doesn't even pay me the measly fourteen grand they owed me.

I consider bringing charges against them, which would kill the project, I know. I hope the project doesn't work, to be completely honest. I've not seen the product on the road, and it's very visible if it is, so I'm reasonably sure it never hit.

So I do the only logical thing I can do, which is to get the fuck out and lock myself in my apartment for a month with the shades drawn. I eat very little. My buddy Brandon, with whom I went on the cruise, leaves me groceries that slowly rot on the countertop. Then one day, I say that's it, I'm out. I sell everything I own, hop in my unfortunately pimped-out Civic, and drive across the country for five months.

I meet a waitress in Reno, who quits her job that day, and drives with me for four months. We wake up in the mornings and say things like, "Hey, you want to go to Yellowstone today? What about Seattle?"

The whole time I'm programming stuff, and I hate life, but it's a grand experience. I'm utterly distraught, yet I'm having the best adventure, which is some contradiction. Then one day, I get a call out of the blue from some guy who asks if I want to work in corporate again.

This call spins out into four years of corporate insanity, and that's when I lose all interest with anything having to do with corporate. I'll never again be driven for another bland company after those four years and will always be half in after that.

Then I work with a rad startup that's bringing inventions to life for normal people. There are maybe fifty of us when we started, and we hit it hard. We put product after product on the market, including five Internet of Things (IoT) products over the course of six months. I got to lead an amazing team of engineers, who are still my friends today.

Movin' on up.

Once the growth hit at this startup, it's my job to help interview a bunch of potential CTOs, and they're all good except this one guy, we'll call "Silicon Valley Hipster Dick." You guessed it: he's the one they hire, and naturally, he demotes me immediately. One of the other people in the post-review got to be good buddies with him and told him what I said about him.

If you haven't noticed, I don't have a filter. I'm reasonably sure I called him exactly what he heard I called him, and when he demotes me to "Principal Hacker" from "Lead Electrical Engineer," I'm out.

The top electronic device manufacturer in the world at the time calls me randomly and asks if I want to come work for them, but I'm not sure. You know, that whole corporate thing. But when they ask if I want to come work for them for *this much money*, it's yes because I now hate my job, so let's do this. Oh, and money. Right. All good things start by focusing on that…right? Right?!

My first week there is the moment I know I never want to do this again. It's finally the snapping point where I know I never ever want to be in an office and build crap for people again. I draw a calendar in my grid notebook on the first page. I list every workday, and every day off to the exact day, I will vest this stock or that bonus they hire me on with.

Every day I come to the office, I cross it off the calendar. On the exact day after twelve months that I vest, I put in my two weeks' notice to get the eff out of here. They ask me to stick around and finish out the project I was doing, and that's where I choose whether to be mature. I choose maturity and stay around for another two months. It's cool; I wait until I know a door will be open, and I still have doors there. If I ever fail miserably, I know I can always go back and start a new calendar.

The whole time I worked there, they knew I owned a small business. What they didn't know was that my company was marketing, fourth-tier, for a competitor. I disclosed everything I was doing and made sure I never put a competitor logo on anything. I made it so my client could upload the logo. I was four people removed, but in my heart, I knew what it was used for. The agency, my client, eventually acquired me for a percentage of their company. That was a rad experience and probably why I was so addicted to the fast-paced, dirty marketing world until burning out.

I'm not sure happiness is even a thing.

Everything you read about psychology says that happiness doesn't exist. Joy does exist, but as a general short-term emotion only. I think the ideal goal is contentment, and contentment for me only happens when I'm in the zone. Contentment slows when I'm in this weird world of social engagement we've created.

When I'm drawing or building cool shit or playing music, I'm in my happy place of joy. And then I come back here, to the "real world," I have to deal with my taxes, a system made up by a bunch of people I've never met. Or I'm listening to somebody's baby daddy drama. In other words, I'm dealing with strife.

My goal is contentment, which is being in the zone, and being in the zone requires that I have money. Having money enables creating a zone, but I have to strike a balance of being stuck back into the crap I hate to be in that contentment state. I think there's no real happiness, just the continual strife to use as a tool to get back to that place you want to be.

If I have to take my car and get it fixed because I got stuck in a sandstorm, well, that's a nuisance. I'm getting my car back to the status quo, but I'm not getting a Ferrari out of the deal. I spent three hours on the phone to get my car cleaned. But strife is interesting in that during the strife of having my car returned to its previous state, I'm content. Yes, in America, strife is often a phone call. Tough life, eh?

Strife might suck, but I've always embraced it. I enjoy the search for solution after solution, as it keeps me busy. Something I learned years ago was that when you're racing cars, you don't freak out. You might flip, roll, run into a wall, go 130 or 160 mph, but you can't freak out. The second you get back on the paddock and pull that car over, you can yell, scream, cry, or freak out all you want. But not in the moment.

The key to strife is that when you're in that strife moment, you're not crying, "Woe is me!" You're saying, "Let's solve this thing first, and let's cry when we get home." Strife is a form of contentment that drives you to do better things; it drives you to dig out.

A world populated by clones of me.

Clones of me would be uniquely terrible. Pardon the inverse pun. I'm pretty sure I would hate and love myself. I feel like it would be a lot of people driven by strife, pushing each other to be better, to see who's the fastest, who can work the hardest, who can ignore the most useless things.

Who wants to do things like register your car? What a nuisance and a total waste of time! My car still works without a registration, it turns, it moves, it lights up. Or jury duty. While it's not a waste of time, it is, because there are so many things like that which detract. I actually have jury duty coming up, but I lost that letter. I don't get the mail more than once a month.

If the world were full of clones of me, many boring things would not happen. The world would fall apart. The IRS would go bankrupt. The trash would never be wheeled out to the curb.

The flip side would be that there would be a bunch of people who are passionate and motivated. There would be a lot more ideation, a lot more prototyping. I think you would see a plethora of inventing, but not as much follow-through on stupid ideas.

We wouldn't have as much trash laying around, and by trash, I mean toy frogs for the carnival. We'd think, *That's a cool stupid toy, but we're not going to manufacture it because it's a waste of time.* You would see much more focus on innovating and much less focus on payday loans or money-making schemes. There would be no time for pyramid schemes.

But I don't think we would focus enough on the money. You must have money-focused people, and our world would be based solely on build, which would lose balance in other places.

Oh, and nobody would have kids, so it'd be one short-lived generation. But then again, we could keep making more clones.

II

Personal Principles

Ethics

All work and no play makes Jack a dull boy.

I work hard, and I also travel hard, but even vacations are work. Everything in your head is work when you're like me. I just came off seven weeks of work and travel, and I knew I should have stopped after three, but I didn't. My girlfriend and I were hiking in Guatemala, and she said, "We should quit," and I said, "No, we're going to see where this ends." And I got dehydrated and dizzy, but I kept going to see where it would end.

That's how my life goes.

At any given moment, I'm driven. I may be exhausted, but there's always another day to keep pushing, and things keep stacking one on top of the other. My trip was supposed to end after three and a half weeks, but then it turned into four, five, six, and then seven weeks. I'm not sure this aspect of me will ever change. I know this about myself, and when people talk about it, I feel annoyed as I'm not hearing anything new.

Even a vacation isn't always a vacation, so going to Guatemala was the worst decision. I had just come from three weeks of working sixteen-hour days and not sleeping and went right into driving six hours in crazy traffic. We stayed two nights at a hotel, met all these new people, and did all the stuff my girlfriend wanted to do, which didn't work for me because I needed to do my burnout process. I should have known better. It was not her fault in any way; she was just trying to enjoy her vacation.

One rule I have is not stacking up things that sound like a vacation on top of a long build—because everyone knows that vacation is not usually a vacation. You think it will be so relaxing, but the only relaxing vacations are the ones old people have, such as taking a cruise or lying on the beach for seven days. Our generation doesn't go on relaxing vacations. We strive to see as many things as we can in two days and then talk about how great it is on Instagram.

When I was young, all I wanted to do was party, have fun, play metal, hang out with my buddies, go skateboarding, and now the thought of rock climbing turns my stomach. I used to love it, and now I live a mile from one of the best rock-climbing spots in the world. That's why I moved here, but I've worked myself into a place where I don't want to do it anymore.

It's important to take the time to make sure you still love the things you love. I have a list of things I should have done, such as putting more precedence on the people in my life. Now I find my relationships to be a nuisance because they're taking me away from the thing I'm built to do, which is to work. The seventeen-year-old me would not be proud of me sitting here figuring out how to make more money. Yet that's what I do.

This dullness comes from all work and no play. Something that drove me to succeed when I was young, which I'm having trouble with these days, was I always wanted to do the right thing. I wanted to excel. My goal was to build the best products, to build something I was proud of, something I could show people and say this is what I did my best at.

In college, we had to pay to learn, and as soon as we got out of school, we found idiots paying us to learn. I thought, *This is what I want to do, and they're willing to pay me?* That's what made me excel when I was young. I didn't have a regimen. I didn't want to go to dinner with a bunch of people to talk about superfluous crap; I wanted to figure out how this electron could move over here to create data to drive visualizations.

I spent hours on end to get the dimming curve on a little blinker on a car to dim out exactly like an incandescent bulb would in the '20s and '30s. I showed my manager, and I didn't tell him what it was. He said, "That feels nice," and that was what I lived for: the things you couldn't explain, but you could feel.

But once that fire's gone because you've worked too hard, you're screwed. When the fire burns down, you must have rules to succeed. But you're not succeeding like you used to, because that fire was the driver. How do you reignite that fire? By following the burnout ritual I've been perfecting for years.

Here are the rules for the burnout kit.

I plan to be sick, and I plan to be burned out after a long build, so I've created a series of rules for what I call the burnout kit. When I'm burned, I feel nothing. I neither feel joy nor anger. I'm not annoyed; the most annoying thing in the world could happen in front of me, and I'm like okay, cool, whatever. I'm out of emotions, out of energy, out of everything.

The first day you get back from something like a long project or travel, lay on the couch, sick or not, all day. If you're like me, you'll stare at a wall while the TV is on, and you're looking to the left of it. You end up feeling broken, so you have to force yourself to make sure you don't leave dirty dishes around. Make sure you vacuum the carpets and do something else to slowly ramp yourself back up. An object at rest stays at rest.

If you're going to be good for the next round of this thing, you can't drink and do hard drugs at that point. So if I'm going to drink, party, and have a great time, it has to be during the middle of a burn or a build. That keeps it isolated. I've found you can spend two or three months drinking and messing up your life because you're so burned out, and you let that be where you stay.

The first rule to get back on track is to go to bed at a reasonable time. Force yourself to sleep, or you'll sit on the couch and watch dumb movies all day and night. Another corresponding rule is that the TV can't be on more than half the day.

Start setting the time you'll permit yourself to do each activity. My rule, for instance, is no marijuana until the end of the workday, even if it's not a workday. When I'm in burnout mode, from the time I wake until 5:00 p.m., I can't smoke weed. I can't have a beer because that will end my day immediately. I'm burned out, so what else am I going to do? I'll sit there and drink eight beers in the next two hours and go to ruin. If I start at 5:00 p.m., then I won't feel so terrible the next morning.

Another rule is no engagements for three full days. I broke this rule this last time around. I had my girlfriend over, and it went horribly awry because I got sick of her when, generally, I never get sick of her. I quickly got tired of her talking because I wanted to zone out in silence. I worked too hard; I put myself in a bind, and I needed to be able to nurse myself back to health.

If you haven't felt that way before, then you're probably not going to understand. You will sit there and complain that I only talked to you once in fifteen minutes, and I don't want to have to explain why I need to be alone for two days. I need that quiet. I've been listening to people talk and tell me why 5 percent of my product sucks—when 95 percent is good—for the past seven weeks.

My set of rules gets that fire back, which I lost by working too hard and out of balance. I think in my head I can dive right back into it, but I can't when I'm burned out. I can't spend three days relaxing, and then it's right back to work on the next product. I need a balance with a normal life. If I can't do moderation, I need to calculate how much time normal people take off versus how much time they work. If the average person works thirty-two hours a week, and that's their happiness point, and you worked eighty-hour weeks for three months, you need to take three or four months off to heal.

I've been running myself ragged for small projects because I think I need the money. But I could do fewer small projects and do some nice big projects, make more money, plus feel happier and more aligned. You need that mathematical capacity to maintain balance even when different swings occur.

As I get older, I look at a longer-term picture that involves being slightly colder. When you're a nice guy, and everybody comes to you with their dreams, it's hard to tell them you don't want to help with their dreams. But I was burning out doing thirty hours a week on pro bono projects, so when I cut those out completely, then I was much happier.

My pro bono clients have their dreams, but I also have my own dreams, and I need to chase them. I've taken on a lot of projects for super cool people because I wanted to hang out with them. But then I was losing my mind because it's their dream, not mine. Time is the most precious thing we have, and now that's the thing I would be least likely to give up. I'd rather donate money than give my time to a random project.

Another important thing to do is planning. If I know I have this burnout period coming afterward, I know I will need three or five days alone. So I push all the scheduling back; anything I can push, I push. While I still haven't perfected the burnout process, I understand that it has to happen. It's about self-awareness, such as building the burnout routine and planning the short and long-term that seems to be what works for me.

Another one in the burnout kit I learned was when I went on a road trip in burnout mode, and I was very angry and fighting with my road trip buddy. I don't know why she put up with me because I was a real Negative Nancy. And then I put headphones in, and I was happy immediately.

Music.

If I can have music or that thing that helps me get in that mode, I forget, and if I listen, then life is fine again. I'm in my happy place, listening to fast-paced music and being quiet. That's my psychology of harmonics. They've shown that sound waves help, but that has nothing to do with it: it's finding that thing that calms me and puts me in that place. Maybe it's painting, writing, or drawing, but there's that thing for everybody that fixes their mood and brings them to that happy place.

Here are methods for finding balance.

Listening to yourself is the key to achieving balance. Know that patches or Band-Aids such as drugs won't help. If you worked a fourteen-hour day, and you think drinking your face-off with your buddies sounds great, it's because you missed so much life. Go home and go to bed. Take a day off, and do something you love.

I worked at a startup in New York, and we would come in hungover at around ten in the morning and work until midnight. Then we'd go out to the bars in New York until they closed at four. I fell asleep in a subway station more than once. I fell asleep on the side of the road a few times too. I vaguely recall some people from Holland helping me go the extra two blocks to my hotel as I threw up. I got off one job after not having slept for three days straight. I finally asked a stranger on the street to walk with me the block and a half back to my apartment, because I was afraid I'd pass out in downtown Los Angeles and someone would steal all my stuff.

When my girlfriend came to New York to visit a site once, she said, "This is crazy! These people don't care about you. They don't care if you die. You're sick and falling apart, and they're mad you're not pulling off this impossible task they gave you. This is an unplanned nightmare." These aren't good places to be, but people like me keep doing it. It's the culture of the startup life, but you need to know when to say no.

I agree to do things I honestly don't want to do. One example is visiting my family, as I never want to do that. It's not that I don't love my family, but I'm looking at a thousand dollars spent and three days of not working. But if it's on the calendar, it forces me to get out and make it happen, but I'm cranky the whole way there. But when I get there, I'm super stoked to be with them.

I've had to design a few methods that help me find balance in this kind of life, such as planning, as I know I tend to overwork. If I'm not working, sometimes I'd rather sit at home on the couch and do nothing because then I'm not burning funds, I lack energy, and it costs just time. This and other things can be avoided just by planning balance into your normal life.

The other thing I've been known to do to find balance is get up and leave, as I did a couple of years ago. Things got to where I'd wake up in my office and work all day, go to bed at 2:00 a.m., roll off the futon at 7:00 a.m., do it again, go, go, go, and I finally found myself angry, bitter, and terrible. So I got up and moved to Nicaragua. Maybe it wasn't the best plan, but I'd rented out my house, and I was sleeping on a couch at the office.

Leaving helped me, and it was exciting for a little while. I saw a different world, and it changed my thinking. I put myself in a place where other people were lackadaisical and fun and could have that thing I felt I wanted. There were a good three or four weeks where I was jazzed to be around all these surfers. All they wanted to do was catch the next wave and have fun and party with each other and fornicate a lot. When I left Nicaragua, I traveled around Europe all year.

You have to force yourself to do these things, or they won't happen. If you're a hustler, you'll hustle all the time, so you've got to force yourself to enjoy the fruits of your labor, even if you're not enjoying it. I understand this struggle intimately and can speak from experience.

I remember sitting with my computer on the prettiest beach I'd ever seen in Portugal, grumbling at the girl I was with because I wanted to work and not rest on the beach. But having that time took me out of that dark place and back into a place where I could work again. When you're young and in your twenties, you can dwell over two or three years like this. It's the startup life. *Go, go, go, go.* Take a day and a half and drink, and then you're fine again.

Around the age of twenty-nine, that stops working. I can't do sixteen-hour shifts every day after that age. I also can't recover as quickly from partying. When you hit twenty-nine, you need two days to recover from a hangover whereas before it was, "Let's drink til the morning then go to Taco Bell, and we're back on track."

This is not a sustainable life, so forcing yourself to create those downtime moments makes sense. A seven-week burn I'm complaining about here on the last round wasn't really that long. That was short for me, and at the end of it, I tried to tell my girlfriend not to come over because I needed to be home alone. I needed the quiet. I knew I would be sick because I'm always sick after those trips, which is interesting and weird; the second I relax, I get sick. I'm used to this.

How to say no.

You have to learn how to say, "No, I don't want to work another fourteen-hour day even though everyone else is." With one crew in NYC, it was about 5:00 p.m., and while I'd already worked an eight-hour day, they were still having freak-out problems. Problems due to their poor planning and ignorance. I charge them a day rate that gets ruined by the time I put in ten hours, and I'm sick out of my mind from no sleep and travel, so I say, "I'm sick. I'm going back to the hotel." And that's that.

The client looks shocked. "Okay, feel better," he says, but he looks like a deer in the headlights. He clearly doesn't expect me to bail out, but I do just that. I don't expect them to hire me again as I know they're upset with me. The next day, he says, "Well, dude, it seems like you're getting weak in your old age."

Ha.

It's not worth it anymore to me. They call me every day with a problem, and finally, I say, "You guys rushed the project. I told you not to. You called me to triage things. I don't intend triage fixes to be long-term." Now I charge them hourly whenever they call.

They'll try to replace me, as they've done this twice before. They'll call me back in two months when the other suppliers quit or are fired, and this time, I'll overcharge them, again. This is the second time I've said no to them. I always tell them to find a new supplier. I've never yelled at anybody on the phone, but I once yelled at them because they messed up a project and tried to blame me.

I later took the time to warn the owner of issues, to which he was a complete dick, so it's a no-win. My father always told me, "You can't argue with crazy," and I've found that bullies are crazy. You will always be wrong.

I've found that when you don't say no, you turn into a kitten. It's a curve where you go full force, you've got the fire, you're doing a great job, you're on point, and then once you burn yourself out, you become a kitten. You get walked on. You lose your strength by working too hard. You lose your ability to say no until all you can utter is a small, defeated *no*. The sick no wasn't a strong no. It wasn't a no like the other one where I said, "This is not how you treat suppliers. Find yourself a new electronics supplier."

You can't be afraid of conflict. What we do is full of conflict, and to embrace what we do, you must be able to fight— not having a disrespectful fight, but rather embracing that conflict. You can get to that point—well, one more thing, and you're a kitten because you don't have the energy to fight. It's much easier to sit there and solder a wire than to engage in a conflict.

Be on your A game; don't work yourself ragged and become the kitten. Once that happens, you're a tool, and you're being pointed and aimed. Have the fire, have that focus. For me, if I want to build something, and that's my focus, then I have to be strong enough to choose what I want to build. I have to be able to say, "No, it's not worth my time. Your project will not bring me happiness." But to be in that place, be strong and have confidence that you're not so burned out you can't make things happen on the other side.

For any small business owner, it's hard to say no to a project, because you're not sure if there will be more projects, or if you'll even have the energy to take them on. So even though this one might suck, I take it. I've got to pay the bills because I might not have energy. But if I didn't take that, and if I didn't go to New York with a cold, I would've been better prepared to fight for something bigger. I could keep running myself ragged over pennies when the reality is that I can hunker down for three months and make half a million dollars. But I should stop chasing one or two-thousand-dollar days. It's key to watch for that slip, that digression of being weak.

When I found my burnout happening out in Guatemala, I was fine at first. It seemed like a mediocre idea to drive four and a half hours up to Lake Atitlan to check out Mayan shit when I should have been stoked to go up there and check this thing out. But I didn't want to do it. I just wanted to sit on the beach, but I gave in. I didn't want to argue and experience my girlfriend being upset with me while on vacation (rightly so). But if I truly felt I didn't want to go, I should have had the strength to say so.

You always have that moment where you realize you're swallowing your feelings, and that's always that point where you will be weak. Following that vacation, I came home and did a project for five days straight. Then we went out to June Lake, which was a rough Thanksgiving during burnout. Just awful. I was burning out with two kids screaming around me.

Directly back from that, I had six hours to pack and fly to Miami. I got back and had one day to repack and get to New York while suffering a cold. But at that moment where I didn't want to check out the Mayan ruins, I shouldn't have kittened out. I should have said I wasn't going, but I didn't. That's not a winner of a story, but that's how you know that the thing you want to do is the one you don't want to do. But you give in because you don't want to deal with listening to somebody talk. Plus, the Mayan ruins are amazing, and I should've enjoyed them in person, properly.

Healthy boundaries in a relationship.

Establishing boundaries is always going to be a feeling; there's not a metric for that. There will be a moment where your heart wrenches, and you know a word or action wasn't nice or thoughtful. Then you argue, they argue back, and you realize this person is a dick. And the moment you give in to something you're not comfortable with, that's when you know.

Nobody cares about you in business—they care about what you can deliver. You've got a few friends here and there that'll take some hits, but generally, they're not your friends, so you can't blame the other person. This is business. You can't say that that person is using me; it's whether or not you're allowing yourself to be used.

We can't get into the blame cycle because the blame cycle's always going to be a mess. Everything that happens to you is going to come down to having made a poor decision and your own fault. When you try to blame others, it's usually you that put yourself in that situation. You could have safely sat it out and never dealt with the pain, but you didn't, so it's your fault.

When I was a kid and did something wrong and tried to blame others, my dad used to ask me, "Boy, is there a ring in your nose?"

"No."

"Then nobody made you do that."

Avoid breaking yourself for a relationship. Listen to yourself, and don't get into situations where you feel uncomfortable and reach a point where you're so weak you don't have the strength of character to say no. That's on you as well; if you know you're feeling weak, then you should withdraw for a bit. Get your strength back, however you do so. Maybe it's as simple as enjoying hot chocolate with marshmallows. I don't care how you do it, but get your strength back because you can't kitten out and blame somebody else for your failures.

My uncle was putting furniture in a casino, and at the end of the install, Donald Trump said, "Great. The cabinets look beautiful." It was a big job, and my uncle installed some fine furniture. Trump said, "I'll pay you 10 percent." The story isn't crazy, as Trump is a businessman, and that's what he does.

But my uncle said, "There's no problem if you can't pay for the install. I'll have my guys come tomorrow, and you can pay the 10 percent for the labor, and we'll pull those cabinets out. That's cool." My uncle got his full tab for the deal.

Many people would have settled because they needed that money. My uncle probably needed it too, but he had the strength of character to say he would not get walked on. If Trump wanted my uncle to install his cabinets, then Trump had to pay for it. Installing that furniture was a huge job for a small guy like my uncle. It would have put him out of business if Trump had only paid him 10 percent of his fees. Would you be willing to do that in your life?

I admire Nikola Tesla. When his buddy Westinghouse was in a bind for money and trying to get AC out there, Tesla would have been the richest man in history had he kept the contract on his amount per kilowatt-hour. But he gave that up because he wanted the technology to better humanity. He was all about the best for everybody and science. He never cared about politics. Edison was a cutthroat asshole who wasn't as scientifically brilliant. Nikola is on the other side and didn't care whose name was on the project. He just wanted it to be right, and I respect that.

Even when we're burning out, we should carry ourselves with class and dignity. Frank Sinatra kept his skeletons in the closet, for example. Rumors are good, and maybe people assuming you're linked up with gangsters is a good thing. But if you're saying you're linked with gangsters, that's not a good look. Somehow, Sinatra's records ended up in every upstanding home, yet everybody knew he was smoking, drinking, womanizing, and having lunch with Al Capone's fam. But none of these rumors were things that he came out and said himself.

I saw an executive at a company recently who I thought didn't like me. He wanted to hear my story because he said I carried myself with composure, even in crazy situations. I was the only one on-site who was fixing the display quietly without moving quickly. I liked his compliment, and that meant a lot to me. You want people to see that even in crazy situations, you remain calm, but you also solve things fast.

When you're freaking out, you make a lot of mistakes. But when you sit down and spend fifteen minutes in the middle of the war to ask yourself how to solve this problem, then you've struck that balance. At the very least, have that outward appearance as people who maintain composure do better work.

I think our generation likes the haggard look, and we're all proud of each other for being haggard. But being and looking good has pushed my career further than it would have if I were looking like every other startup person. You don't always get along with the other startup people better, but the people above notice you move faster and still look composed. So the camaraderie sometimes falls away, as the others think you're not suffering like the other people, but you are. You're just suffering a little more to look like you're suffering less.

Flow

Don't underestimate the importance of a flow state.

Flow is that moment when you go from learning how to snowboard, like controlling your balance and being afraid of a bump in the snow, to when you put on your headphones and feel one with the white mountains. Flow is where everything becomes muscle memory, and everything else falls away.

It's akin to meditation or LSD. When you're talking to yourself in your head, it's obnoxious to be thinking in words. But in that flow state, you're thinking in pictures. The "front" of your brain is off as you flow, and the monologue stops.

When I write software or do woodworking, I'm not having a monologue with myself; I'm thinking in pictures, thinking about the next step. When I'm in a code set, the world explodes into a 3D plethora of these little boxes with lines between them, and I can zoom in, zoom out, twist, get in there, and immediately feel what's wrong.

When I built circuit boards back in the day, I built complex things by hand without a schematic or a drawing. I would look in my head at the 3D of where the data, electrons, and everything else needs to go, and when I see the picture, four out of five designs would be near-perfect, functionally, on the first shot.

When I'd look at the work of other people not in flow, I'd see umpteen errors in the first design review. It's not that I was any better, technically, as these other people knew more than I did. They knew many more shortcuts and were probably smarter, but for them, it was a conversation about this goes here and then that goes here. With me, it was art.

That flow state takes you from math to feeling, from thinking and asking to allowing your brain and your muscles to work together. That flow state clears everything. If my mind is not in a flow state for a few days, I become angry and evil. Music is one thing that gives me a partial reprieve, but after spending two hours working on the motorcycle, the world's okay again: reality is gone. Any argument I'm having with friends or girlfriends is gone. I'm not worried about her being angry or the consequence of my actions. I'm there, and I'm fully present.

You can't hate on somebody if you're happy. When you're in a flow proper, it feels like a lucid dream you control. It's a good feeling; a mute thing. When you know a wire's missing in the design, it's a bad feeling that pokes at you and tells you that something is wrong. The excitement you feel on the other side is amazing. It's the same as when you finally hit that meditative state and you're more or less lucid dreaming, and you control it.

Study Richard Feynman's experiments, and you'll learn that when he dreamed, he tried to stay awake. I mean, he scared the crap out of himself, so that says something. Try when you're falling asleep not to lose your dialogue. It takes a week or two, but at some point, your brain starts lucid dreaming. You've got 3D things going on as your brain is drawing instead of trying to remember your drawing, but then you're still thinking.

There's a parallel between a happy and a flow state. When your brain draws, it's magical. If you spend too much time in reality, you will be unhappy and trashy. Sad but true. When you feel terrible, angry, and irritable, it probably means you didn't use your brain to disappear from reality and get into a flow state.

When you're thinking with the "front" of your brain, you're not very good at stuff, but when you disappear into that world where two hours feel like three minutes, that's flow. It can be as simple as putting on your headphones to jam for a bit and coming out on the other side feeling alive and refreshed.

I'm not a habitual person. In fact, I don't think there's a single thing I do every day, except maybe eating and moving. There's this dogma around successful people and leaders that it's all about routine and structure. While this can inspire people struggling with a way to find success, my take is that you don't need a routine: you need flow.

It would make me happier to feel that drive or structure or habit, but it's not me. Moving quickly and being good at what I do relies on me enjoying the process. I'm more of an artist than an engineer: my art is building apps. And as an artist, I need to be in the right mode.

I can't say that at nine thirty I will start coding, or I will wake up and do yoga every morning. To me, that's work. If I want to practice Spanish, I do it daily, but I don't do it at the right times; I do it when I have the time. So while I'd love to be at one with the calendar, I'm not. If someone needs to reschedule a meeting, I'm never upset. It will happen when it happens, and we're both going to enjoy it. This lack of routine has driven me to connect with my flow and find ways to on-ramp when I need to do so. These on-ramps into flow or flow triggers—to use the pop terminology—work well for me.

Music.

I will avoid the scientific research about flow, as that's well above my paygrade, but pairing music with an activity or a mindset is key to flow for me. It isn't pairing any music with what you're doing but adding the correct music to the task at hand. And I would even argue it's down to the correct song, album, or artist to pair with what you're doing.

The job of a developer is isolated, so early on, music became a big friend of mine. When I'm working twelve or sixteen-hour days, I'm deep in thought the entire time. Music is the only thing I can do that's not work, so I live in a world of music for five, six, seven days a week.

I learned this trick years ago while working on automotive designs one night about eleven when I still had so much work to do. The first song of Trivium's *In Waves* album came on, and I zoned in. As soon as the entire beat dropped out and then hit hard again with screams, I put my head down and started coding, and the next thing, I knew it was morning—time had been distorted.

We have a bunch of trails in the desert where I live. I've got an old Willys Jeep for the big stuff, plus a Subaru Impreza WRX that goes fast off-road. When I'm getting ready to get into a flow to run a lap or just to head to the gas station (and it's usually way too fast), I put on the song "Wonderful Life" by Bring Me The Horizon because I'm a bit of a closet metalhead.

I've discovered that it takes transitional songs for me to trigger a flow state. "Wonderful Life" starts out with a calm, kind of talky intro, and then it hits hard and fast-paced afterward. It provides for a clean transition from a loose mental state into a drop into another world: the guitar hits, and the lead screams, and I'm in a flow.

If I'm a touch depressed, as soon as the song hits the hard, drop part, then I'm thinking about the guitar. What I'm not thinking about is the world around me, the drama, the details, the messiness of life. The problem with that song is that I'm jarred back to reality at the end, which requires a quick flip around the track to rejoin the world. For me, that song's more of an ephemeral, quick moment away from the world—an island of flow if you will.

I listen to a lot of metal when I do things that require a flow state. When I'm preparing to take on a bigger project, I listen to a full album, not just a song. Again, I listen to something like the album *In Waves* by Trivium. The intro to that album is the centerpiece of that drop into the flow. The entire thing crescendos into this massive song, layering in piece by piece. It has a piano, then builds in with an electric guitar in a calming, methodical manner. It was also my first.

When I know I need to work hard on something with a lot of detail, I close my eyes, take my song out, put my fingers together, and notice every detail. I listen to the guitar come in; I listen to the beats and let it incrementally take me from wherever I am into fully focusing on the intro building.

At the end of the intro when that silence happens, I open my eyes, put my glasses on, and immediately it hits, and there's the screaming and metal. And then it's just me, the computer, and this endless, fast runway of beats. The singer has an even keel scream that works when I'm building something; he's not swearing at me. There's no intrusion, just an expert vocalist that moves and keeps me going; I focus on the music and flow and then allow that to carry me to another place.

Some music brings me up. For instance, if I listen to Frank Sinatra in the morning, it puts me into the best mood in the world. But then, as all things do, it has to balance out, so by the afternoon, I won't be in a great mood. I've got emotion on both sides of that because the afternoon is not as good as the morning. And when I'm in this great emotional state, it's hard to focus and be one with whatever I'm doing. I won't listen to Frank Sinatra in the morning because it makes me *too* happy. I can't focus when I'm happy, but then again, I can't focus when I'm sad or angry either.

The biggest key to getting into a flow that I've found is to know the music, and I know it well. When Justin Bieber's song "Love Yourself" came out, I had to listen repeatedly, because the first ten or twenty times I heard it, the music distracted me. I've been listening to Trivium for a long time, so it's easy for me to get into the flow state. If I want to introduce something new, I need to listen to it while traveling or some other mundane task before it becomes my flow state music. At the airport, for example, I'll listen to the new bands on repeat that I plan to shift into my workflow.

Music is a personal wallpaper, and I often like to redecorate that room. I'll have an album or a song run on repeat for a month straight, but once in a while, it needs to shift. I can't live with that same wallpaper all the time. I think playlists are fun, but I find them jarring when they shift personality. It's not just about the genre, but the overall fabric of the music should be relatively even between pieces, which is why I prefer a full album. I don't even like to switch albums between the same bands or musicians because the style of progression, or the timbre of the voice changes if the singer was swapped out, which can be grating.

I find timbre is key. Even if the beat shifts, the same artists have the same styles, such as the drummer has maybe five patterns he plays and changes around. It might slow down here and there, but there's some thread tying it all together, so you're not changing your wallpaper. For example, I can listen to The Used and Thursday because their vocals are close, but if I go from The Used to A Skylit Drive, then I've changed my entire world; I changed the wallpaper, and I'm no longer focused.

Often I listen to the same song or album on repeat for days on end, and it can be the same song sometimes. I'm not paying attention to it. It doesn't get boring because it's not like watching the same movie over and over. I'm creating an environment. And once I find the proper noise to create with, I want that environment to be known and static. No surprises, as I want to know the next song that will play. I already know the words to that beautiful wallpaper to the environment I created.

In this case, the music is a tool, a background. It's something I hear but don't listen to. It's not a focal point. So I listen to fast-paced music, and I listen to it loudly. At one point, I was working at a headphone company, and we had the best, newest headphones because that's what we were working on. A coworker shot me with a Nerf gun, and I took my headphones off, and he said, "It's the weirdest thing. You type quickly, but you're typing to the beat of the music you're listening to."

"How do you know?"

"'Cause your music's too loud."

He was trying to complain to me, but what I took away was I ended up in this place where my head is moving, fingers typing, foot tapping; I'm rocking back and forth, and my mind shuts up and goes. I don't mean to tap to the beat, but I've noticed this in the years since. Whenever I'm fully in flow, my fingers are playing a keyboard, but I'm playing the letters I'm typing. And once I can get to that point where the monologue—that inner stupid, annoying voice always talking to me—dies, the flow state takes over.

Music is the easiest way in the door as it shuts out the rest of the world. You can meditate in pure silence and get to that place. But if there's one little tick noise from the air conditioner, you're kicked out of a flow. When you're blasting metal, you can't hear anything. I hated metal as a kid, but I learned to love it because that's my way of getting into a flow.

Being ADD, anything will distract me. Music cuts off my ears and creates a safe space.

Make sure you have a one-to-one relationship with whatever you're doing. For me, repetitive patterns will move me into a flow state, such as snowboarding and rock climbing. When your mind is busy with *this hand, that hand, this hand, that hand*, or *that hill, this hill, that hill, this hill*, you get in a flow. You're one with the rock or the mountain, and next thing you know you're reading the mountain instead of thinking about the mountain.

Do whatever it takes to shut down the outside world so you're point-to-point with the task at hand. It's you and what you're doing, and that's it. However you can find your flow, go for it. I have a lot of friends who find that yoga or meditation does it for them. They're in tune with their body, so they can get into the flow that way. That inner monologue works for many people to find that dedicated absorption that comes down to only you and whatever you're doing.

Risk.

While risk is a frequent, potent flow trigger for most, you can get into a flow with things you're naturally good at, but when risk enters the picture, that's an *advanced* flow state. If you're not comfortable with what you're doing, then you will think about the risks. However, if you're confident, you'll have no fears before you. It allows you the luxury of knowing that failure is not an option.

Often, knowing you can bow out of something if it fails means you're not getting fully invested, and you're not in that flow state. But as soon as you engage the thought you absolutely cannot fail, you're in an advanced flow. That could be something like rock climbing. Or in my case, I can enter the risk zone knowing that if a particular project fails, my business is doomed because we're small.

There's this rock-climbing route out in the park called Sexy Grandma (yes, the name makes me giggle), and I've run it many times. When I was younger, I ran up in a full flow without thinking. Zip, zip, zip, zip, and I'm at the top. But that same route now puts me off as I learned I have Meniere's disease, which means I get vertigo quite frequently.

Even if I don't have vertigo on a given day, I doubt my balance now that I know I have Meniere's. I've had it for years, and it never impacted me before as long as I wasn't feeling woozy or like I was falling off a cliff while standing on the ground. But now I expect that to happen when I'm halfway up the route, and I can't get in that flow state because I doubt myself.

While risk can be a trigger to get into a flow state, it can also be a hindrance—it's a hundred percent based on my confidence in myself and the tools at hand. When I'm in the dirt in my WRX, and I have full faith in the vehicle, I can drift as hard as I can, corner to corner, outside, inside, outside. Pulling a string through the course, knowing full well that the car will do what it's supposed to, and I'll tell her the correct maneuver.

However, if I know that the tie-rod is a bit wobbly, I won't drive well; I won't be flowing. As I go into that corner, I'll be thinking, *How do I not press on that tie-rod so that my tire doesn't turn inward and tuck under the car?* Risk is an amazing trigger to get you there quickly, but you must be confident in yourself and your tools.

I've been trying to teach my girlfriend how to drift out and play, how to go from one path to the next side, swipe it, and read the road without actively thinking what the car will do. She's an amazing girl, brutally driven, and smart as a whip. Did I mention I think she's gorgeous, especially when she smiles?

Yesterday, I went down one path, and the car was going in a straight line, but I had the wheels hard turned forty-five degrees to the left, and we're going straight, and I'm not even thinking about it: the car is doing what I want it to do.

But when my she does the same thing, we slip and slide and fall, because she's fighting it out and thinking about what she's doing. She's not comfortable or in flow. She can't drift when she doesn't feel she has control over the car. Whereas when I'm drifting, I feel fully that the car will do what I want.

Learning through risk.

When I'm twelve years old, my dad takes me out in my grand-father's '92 Chevy Silverado to the river bottom near where my grandparents live in Missouri. He teaches me about the gas, the brakes, and how to square corners on gravel going altogether too fast. He says, "If you want to learn to drive at high speed, know how to drive at low speed in the dirt."

We spin out many times, and he says, "Outside of the corner, bud. Okay, brake, brake. Now don't touch those brakes in the corner, now I want that back end spinning! Floor it! Floor it! Okay, I know you're scared. But we will do this again and again until you're not scared and until you're not thinking."

And we do that, over and over.

He teaches me to expect the road to do what you don't expect. A bump in the road doesn't mean you should be scared and adjust, but that you should fly through it like flying an airplane. Don't fight the turbulence, float through it. Don't look at what's happening, but be proactive instead of reactive.

My father teaches me to drive a stick. He says, "Okay, foot at 1,500 RPM, foot at 500 RPM. Okay, stay there. Back to 1,500. Now 4,000. Now 3,500. Now stay, now stay, now stay." I'm annoyed because I want to drive, and I want to drive fast, but he teaches me how to know what the vehicle is doing.

Due to his instruction, I don't even have to look at my RPM when I drive. I can tell what's going on by sound, feel, and where my foot is on the gas pedal. And when I build motorcycles, I take all the gauges off because I can feel the vehicle, and I can feel the road. I help myself get into a flow state with the vehicles I build by removing everything but me and the machine knowing each other by vibration.

I can put on my headphones and know my car by what I feel in my right foot, by what I feel in my ass on the seat. Thanks to my father for taking it out of the realm of my mind and into my body, the back of my brain, and my subconscious; I know that to have a relationship with a vehicle is not to drive but to be a unit.

Risk isn't too much of a factor or trigger I rely on to get into a flow state. It's an in or an out; it's less of a trigger and more of a binary decision. If there's risk involved, and there's any lack of confidence, you can't flow, which means you have to trust. I don't find risk to be a trigger but a driver in either: easier or harder.

However, a flow state that comes out of risk is much more important, hands down. You take the course as fast as you can. You feel your tailpipes scrape on a rock at the edge of the road. You don't break off anything that you hit that's a half an inch into the vehicle. You're stoked that you hit something with a half inch, because that means you're right in the zone.

I can't think of any other flow state where you scream in joy at the end, except with risk. Where you're next to a four-hundred-foot cliff with your Jeep at a diagonal angle, and you pull it through by thinking and minor movements, and at the end, you just let out a howl, it's the most rewarding flow state I can imagine. It's very animalistic. You understand why some people like being in battle. There's nothing more life-affirming than the possibility of death.

It's a better reward, not a guaranteed flow.

Environment: A Group Flow.

In engineering, working with the most competent people in a flow state means that together we solve complex problems in short amounts of time. In a meeting, we might be border-line yelling at each other, and you would think we're mad, but we're not. There's no hate, only passion, and afterward, we often go for beers.

I remember yelling at my buddy Stanley and him yelling back at me at the top of our lungs in a glass cage at this startup with people walking by and staring at us.

We yell, yell, yell, yell, yell—and then we solve the problem. We smile, we laugh, and we go out for beers. It's not a fight, but mutual respect: we're agile and passionate about what we're doing, and so we talk louder and louder at each other. We push ideas with our voices.

Nobody says, "You're an idiot," but they might say, "That idea is stupid!"

"Why is my idea stupid?"

"Because of my data!"

"Hmmm. Maybe you're right."

It will be a problem whenever there's an endgame for any one person in the group because when somebody already has the solution in their mind, they will keep coming back to that, and it will hinder the rest. But if we have an agile, mutual respect, then we're all pulling the right answer. Open minds and mutual respect are keys to get into that group flow setting.

An effective group environment that facilitates flow requires not only having mutual respect within the group but also a shared background. The expectation that goals are attainable and aligned in the group is key.

As soon as you put somebody in the room who is not experienced or knowledgeable enough, you doubt their skills and opinions. But if everybody's at the same level, they can argue all day, but it will be respectful. They're not going to poo-poo the person—they'll poo-poo the idea. The challenge level must be high yet proper, because if it's too easy, then people are bored, and if it's too hard, it's frustrating. Beyond what you think you can do, a challenge keeps you interested in that group dynamic.

Things that ruin a flow state.

Interruptions of any kind ruin a flow state. If somebody taps me on the shoulder, it could take me another fifteen to twenty minutes to get back to where I was: reason *numero uno* why I love headphones. It's hard for me to explain to my girlfriend why she can't talk to me about the quick thing she wants to say. I lose half an hour every time somebody says two words to me. So my rule is if I have earbuds in, you don't get my attention unless it's an emergency.

When I was a kid, my dad explained that nine-to-five was a workday, so I was never to call him unless it was an emergency. I thought he was just being a jerk, but when I got older, I understood. Because in coding, if a thing fails, and you can't go on to the next challenge, you're stuck: you need to solve that to get to the bigger goal. You don't want to be hopping over to the phone for something random as it pulls you out of a flow.

You must enjoy your activity to flow; if you're not engaged, a flow is out. When I'm doing a client's project I don't care about, I can't flow. It's like I'm trudging through if my heart isn't in it. In all things, when your heart's in it, you'll be spectacular while the things you do without a flow will be mediocre.

Bodily needs will absolutely knock you out of a flow. I learned to line up multiple drinks when I'm doing something because I don't want to be thirsty. I always use the restroom before I get into a flow. Be prepared, so if it's hot or cold, you'll be comfortable. Layers, layers, layers. Maybe a hoodie and a sport coat—hipster chic. The same goes for pain, such as stomachaches or headaches. When I get into a flow state, I forget I have vertigo, which is super cool. But other bodily discomforts, like a stomachache, I can't get around.

End of a flow state.

I love the flow world. I hate the real world because we're arguing about feelings and emotions, and in the other world, there are no feelings or emotions: there's only you and your thing. The flow world is an addiction. It's a drug. Honestly, I drink way too much when I'm not in that world, but when I'm in there, I don't want to drink—I want to be high on flow. I want nothing but that; it's my drug. Everything else is methadone for having a flow.

At the end of a flow state, there's another state I've found, and that's the honest, glorious moment when your flow state is still going, but you've finished the task. You got to the top of the mountain, and you mantle it and look out over the valley. You're still following that feeling, the bliss state, the postclimax.

That only happens when the goal is high, when it pushes you, and when you attain your clear goal. The whole point of life is to be in that world where you subconsciously leave reality, and you are fulfilled. You get that coder's high, which is like a runner's high. You finish it, and you go *aaaah!* And that's why we work at a flow state.

Opinionated

Strong opinions are ignorant; strong values are key.

I had very strong opinions when I was younger, but I discovered that each one was founded in ignorance, fear, or blind adherence to the teaching of others. No single statement is 100 percent true. You can always shine a flashlight in a room and form a strong opinion, or you can turn the lights on and see the big picture; it's hard to maintain a strong opinion when you see the big picture.

Strong opinions result from how you feel about the outside world. They cause reactive behavior, such as if you don't like someone's face, you treat them poorly. You can tell when you're reacting to an opinion, when you feel that emotional trigger inside you and flow against it. Strong values are more of a proactive set of templates for running against how you interact with the world. Values have little to do with the outside world.

When you have a strong opinion, you can easily be wrong, and whenever you fight hard for something, you're probably not taking in the whole situation. Nothing in the world is black or white; you could call me jaded or apathetic, but I've lost any strong opinions about anything I can't prove.

For example, I don't know if the world's flat or round. I'm pretty darn sure it's round, but I've never been to space, so I will go with the de facto standard that the world is round. But if you took me to space or showed me proof that the world is flat, I wouldn't be destroyed or freak out because it isn't a strong opinion.

How can you be sure that only your faith is correct? There are so many sects just in Christianity, Islam, or Buddhism taken alone. How do you know that your opinion—your chosen belief—is correct? I often hear from other Christians how things are or how they should be interpreted that don't line up with my Christian beliefs, for example. I like to imagine a world where religious fighting doesn't exist, and we peacefully coexist and accept we each have our own path.

A strong opinion leads to arguments bigger than us. We interpret things, and we say, "*I know.*" Having that strong opinion is wrong, but it's not bad to have a feeling. The cancer is when we forget our personal interpretations of our data and that our opinion of the world is based on our experiences. We forget that the experiences of other people can be equally valid.

My father was a religious man while my mother was never religious, but she went along with it. When I was young, the religious community around me led me to believe that gay people were bad; this homophobic Christian community passed that belief system along to me. Frankly, I never understood why it matters if gays want to get married in New Hampshire. If you're a Christian in Michigan, how does that hurt you? The gay people in NH aren't rallying against

Christians into incest in the south…they've got better things to do, like get married, be happy.

I had a friend in college who didn't talk to me for six months after graduation. When we finally spoke again, he said, "I'm sorry, but I was madly in love with you, and I didn't know how to handle that." He was one of those friends I cared a lot about, and he wasn't a bad guy—so why did I think gay people were bad? Because that belief was ingrained in me from a young age, and I accepted it without thinking. I would not have had that friendship had I held onto the opinion that gay people were bad.

If you're stuck in your opinions, you won't listen to the different viewpoints when others speak.

Once again, we meet the difference between hearing and listening, and I've found that to learn, grow, and connect with others, you should listen. Your opinion could put them off guard or change their inputs to your world. The reason for living the way I do is important because you have to avoid making waves if you're surfing. You can't make your own, you're riding the existing waves, which are the surrounding opinions. I've found if you're opinion-less on the outside, you might be seen as weak. But I don't find that's the case; it leaves a lot of doors open for you. Conversely, if you have no values, you are likely weak.

Being Switzerland makes sense: you're financially stable, never at war, and you can focus on the important things, be that having fun or partying. If you're a little strange, and you don't fully understand what the surrounding people are doing in this new world, then throwing your opinions out there can come across like sandpaper. You end up oversharing, or you say something that puts people off. That's why in business they say not to talk about religion or politics: you're there to do a job and get out.

I wear a cross on my necklace, which causes conversation about religion. I can feign it off and say nothing, but I've found it's a positive to what I do. It instills some amount of trust in me. But I'm also not frequenting places where I can be persecuted for my religion. Recently, I was in New York, and a successful C-level executive looks at my necklace and snarks, "Oh, did you find Jesus?"

"He's hiding around every corner," I say.

I know full well he's Jewish as we have talked about his bar mitzvah before. He's brought up religion to me twice on two different jobs, but both times, I laughed it off with a joke. They teach you at top tech companies that if you're ever in an uncomfortable situation, make a joke—especially if the answer is secret. For example, if somebody asks, "Hey, are you working on that new car?" you can say, "Oh, no, it's a spaceship."

It was interesting to have a very serious employer tell me to make jokes. I learned it immediately on orientation day when I came in and waited for HR to make my badge. I sat in a two-hour session where I learned about their privacy policy. I learned the "make a joke" instruction, as they felt it was key for people like me who knew the secret stuff and were super siloed. I was also taught the lingo for finding out if I could share information with the guy next to me about what I was working on.

Opinion: hierarchy is bad.

Going back to my argument with Tara, in which she said we must obey our elders, I still feel that a forced hierarchy is ridiculous. This person reports to that person who reports to the other person, and then there are three idiots in the chain, and now work isn't going well because too many cooks are in the kitchen. Yet forced hierarchy is the standard. When we try to inject our opinion of how it should be into how it is, the response is often, "You can't change the machine from the inside, but it'll change you."

So if you want to surf that world, remember you're surfing a world you're not a part of. There was a time when I said, "Hierarchy is stupid. We're all working here together. It's on everybody to figure out who they want to work with and how." I was the de facto leader of the engineering team at a startup of about 150 people. We didn't have a manager, so I took the lead in charge of engineering. Then they got new investors, including $100 million from an outside source, and suddenly, they had to have a hierarchy in place.

They were hiring for a CTO, which I didn't want. I wanted to continue what I was doing because we were moving products quickly as our team had a great interface. I was young, so I emailed all my friends, the other leads of all the other teams, the CEO, and the management team:

"I'm trying out for the CTO position. I would love it if you would back me up and put in a good word with management."

I knew that with the hierarchy adding a CTO, we would move slower because there would be more layers of bureaucracy to wrangle. We had found something fluid in our engineering team working together, and anytime I pulled somebody with a purely managerial position into that system, I had to answer questions. Management tends to ask questions because they aren't close enough to understand what's happening, and it generally results in an interesting indirection.

We were a hip company, which meant we would bring in somebody hip as a CTO. In my experience, hip people suck at what they do. They're egotistical douchebags—if you want to know how I really feel—and they don't want to sweep floors. But we have to sweep floors to run a company. If you don't know how to do everybody's job and if you're not willing to do it, you will land on problems. Ego ruins everything for all of us, including myself. It takes a minute to learn that, though. Also, it's hard not to have a big ego when you move quickly, and everybody is telling you how great you are.

Well, my email started some drama. I got pulled in with the CEO and head of HR. The CEO said, "This felt like a vote, like you were taking power away. This is my company. This is not a vote. I decide who does what and when."

I said, "I only asked them for a good word."

"Well, now if we don't promote you, we look bad."

"But this is the right way," I said. "This is my opinion of how it should be." Here, I had a strong opinion about the way the world should work. But it's not a case of how it *should* work but how it *does* work. That wasn't a negative opinion, but it was the wrong opinion to share with others at the company.

So the company brings in a new CTO, the only one I recommended against hiring. Immediately, the CTO demoted me from head of electrical engineering to Principal Hacker because he found out I said, "Of all the CTO candidates, he's the worst." People talk, you know. And in his post-interview, we all sat around, and I think my exact words were, "He's another Silicon Valley douchebag lying about his experience. There's no way he did what he did. He may have hired people to do it, but he did not do it himself." He was the only one I said bad things about; this was another time in my life where keeping my opinion to myself made sense because my opinion was strongly opposed.

About the rest of the candidates, I said, "They're pedantic and organized. They understand their business." But none of the other guys were "cool," and he was the one who was. Kinda. Also, kind of a loser. My words came back around to him, and from the day they hired him, he made it his job to make my life hell.

Then he spent some millions of the company's money, likely causing it to go under. But first, he negotiated the sale of part of the company to another company, and then he took a job there. It was shady all the way around as he was a classic bureaucrat. He ran things into the ground and eventually floated to the surface, just like most of the trash in the ocean. And that's Silicon Valley for you.

You can train yourself not to form strong opinions.

Learn what it feels like when you have an opinion about something, because it may not be an opinion. It might be a value, and that's something you can't give up. When your heart twists in disgust, take a moment, because that means you're reacting instead of thinking it through. While the gut is often right, as soon as you feel that opinion welling up, make sure you have all the data. Keep an open mind, and never go to 100 percent on feeling.

For instance, in my *opinion*, I don't like churches. I believe in God, but I have very little interest in spending time with churchgoers or tithing to further a group I frankly don't want to be around. My *value* is that I believe in God, and I believe in his Word and follow his works. But since it's important to me that I don't tithe to a place I have an opinion about, my values conflict with my opinion.

To ease my internal conflict, instead of putting money into a building of bricks and faces, I tithe to those around me. It might be an Uber driver or someone who goes above and beyond and smiles through tough situations. Maybe it's that person who's down on his luck and asks for food instead of money.

I carry around a hundred-dollar bill in my pocket at all times to give away. Sometimes I'll wrap it in a dollar bill, depending on the situation, and make my exit before they can figure out what I've handed them. It's not about a thank-you; it's not about feeling great about myself. It's about following through on my value, which is following my faith. I believe that strong values lead us to be our best in an interfacing sense and affect how we carry ourselves.

Values make your life better.

Values are known truths, such as the golden rule. For example, "murder is bad" is an opinion. "I don't murder" is a value. Opinions are based on interpreted truths and therefore aren't always or necessarily true. For example, I refuse to steal anything. Even if the rest of the world assumes that I steal, I know I don't. And when I do, I rectify it. Therefore, I'm free to live my life without concern on that front. That's an example of where values can make you more confident.

I refuse to lie, but sometimes I do, so I feel the need to clean up my words quickly. Otherwise, they ride on me for a long time because if I know I'm a liar, then I also have to put that brain space in there. I don't cheat on people, which comes down to the heart. Cheating is not only hooking up with somebody; it can also just be thinking about somebody else in a manner you shouldn't.

Avoiding the Seven Deadly Sins is a general goal of mine, and I don't always follow them, but I always try to do so. I wasn't religious growing up, but in my opinion, the rules established by religion are great guides toward the actual truth. People have had thousands of years to figure out what works best, and so even if you take deity out of most religions, you have rules for interaction that are truths. Avoiding these sins helps me keep my life clean as opposed to making other people like me or think I'm a good person.

I had an interesting moment in the mountains. I'd sold everything I owned and was driving around the country, wondering why I felt so empty. I had a good career. I was making a lot of money. My company was doing well. Yet I always felt empty, gross, and horrified. I was jamming my metal songs through this FM transmitter in the mountains, and suddenly, the radio signal overrode when I asked myself, "Why, God, do I feel so empty when I did everything right?" In that instance, my music cut out, and a voice over the radio said, "Because you were doing it for the glory of self, and not the glory of God."

Then it cut back into my music.

I was floored; I had to pull over. It was a coincidence, and I could explain the science of it, but I couldn't explain the timing, and that's something I've sat on and thought about for many years. We can do the right thing, but we can do it for the wrong reasons—ergo, it's still the wrong thing. We can establish rules because we're afraid of punishment, or we can follow the rules because we understand they improve our lives as they are the truths.

I'm not referring to the stupid rules such as you can't swear in front of women and children in Michigan, or you will be fined; I'm talking about the general guidelines that come down to where your heart is. You can do all the right things and still feel empty, so understand why you do them. That's the difference between an opinion such as "The Bible is right" and a value such as "Following the teachings of the Bible improves my life."

I would say that the one value that has made me the happiest and simultaneously the most depressed is taking the time to understand other people. Understanding the perspective of others while putting yours in the backburner allows you to turn the lights on in the room instead of shining a flashlight with your anger. Even in an argument with somebody, try to see their side so you can understand what you're doing and see if it makes sense to talk about it.

If you speak only on the surface, that prevents you from dealing with what's lurking deep down, such as "Hey, I feel lonely," when you're fighting over why somebody is not here right now. The value of taking every person as a human means that their opinions and feelings are valid, and then you can dive into the actual issue.

You can save a lot of time and heartache and maintain your relationships by validating the feelings of others. Yes, you'll take on a lot of sadness for people when you get past the "They're mad I'm not coming to dinner." The strongest value is to understand that people are people, and they're all equal, and their feelings and thoughts are as valid as yours. So take the time to understand them.

Nothing is black or white, everything is a shade of gray.

Tupac said something akin to, "We're all shades of gray. Nothing's black or white." Even in your darkest of dark grays, you should understand there's still some percent of white in there somewhere, and you might be wrong. Take that moment and get used to that feeling where you question yourself if you're judging. Realize you're forming a strong opinion that you can't base in reality.

To put this into context, I was a partner in a company that did a lot of marketing. When I showed up, we did about

$1.2 million in business that year. Two years later, when I left, we were five to six times larger. Part of this was because I ran myself ragged, and another part of this was the team running themselves ragged for me, while the entire time I had a business partner who couldn't do anything right. He only wanted to be in the building with the rest of us. But he wouldn't put in the time, and he was a brat, for lack of a better way to put it. But he also happened to be the CEO.

I spent two years at odds with this guy. He kept trying to do stuff, and he would break things I'd worked on and say, "Well, you can fix it." I thought he was terrible at everything he did, plus he was very mean to the staff. I got so bogged down on how he treated the staff like they were trash and useless and how he was worth everything. He had left an assistant manager position at a cellular phone store to start the company, which made me wonder why he had the hubris at all.

Through all this, I'm thinking he's a bad guy who's not good at anything. This was my perception, but after getting screwed on my buyout through all kinds of contractual messes, I realized he wasn't the idiot I thought he was. He wasn't good at what we were doing, but he was sure good at screwing me over and making sure it protected him. There was a game in the back of all his actions. Every contract that came out put me in a worse position. Due to my perception that he was a fool, I underestimated the entirety of him based on one area.

My perception was he couldn't be good at anything, but he was a mastermind at screwing people over. As I look back, he nailed it. He got people to work for less than minimum wage while paying them slightly more than that over sixteen-hour days and ninety-hour weeks. He'd tell them, "This is a good job. You're making double minimum wage," which isn't true when you're working ninety to or hundred-hour weeks.

Don't write people off because they can still get you. Had I been thinking everyone has a superpower, I would have been looking for his. I had perceived him as a certain thing early on and then went with my perception without taking the time to see him for what he was.

My art teacher used to tell me, "Perceiving is what you see in your head while seeing is what's really there, and seeing is much more important." If I were to ask you to draw a tree, you would draw what you perceive to be a tree. But if I were to ask you to draw that tree I'm pointing at, you would have to see the tree and draw it bark for bark, leaf for leaf.

It's the difference between a still life painting and a Picasso. A Picasso is what he perceived, and a still life painting is what artists see, which is what we call perception bias. When dealing with people, we should see instead of perceiving, or we will put ourselves in a bind. We might write off somebody who's truly a great person or, in the case I described above, misjudge someone who is not a great person.

My grandfather said anti-feminist things, but he was the one who sent my aunt to college and bought her a car to get there even, though he would joke, "Women don't need education." You might *perceive* him as an anti-feminist, but you need to *see* that he was the one enabling his daughter's education.

Everything is real.

Growing up, all I ever wanted was work in Silicon Valley, and when I finally got that job at one of those big companies there, I didn't like it, and it wasn't cool. It wasn't what I saw on *Pirates of Silicon Valley*, where they were having crazy epic office trials. Nope. I went to the coffee machine and then I coded for a bit and then talked to a couple of people, then coded a bit again. When you put people, jobs, and scenarios on a pedestal, you forget they're real.

"I want to be an astronaut," you say. But do you ever think of the years of suffering that go into pursuing that career? There's a story about a fan who yells up to a musician, "Man, I would give my life to play guitar like you!" This musician turns around with angry eyes and says, "You know what? I did give my life to play guitar like this." That's real, so set your expectations accordingly.

I finally got the car of my dreams when I saved up and traded in an RX-7 I had built from parts to buy a Toyota Supra—the car I wanted my entire life. I loved my RX-7, and I knew her inside and out. She was a cheap car, and she was old, but she was fun and pretty and fast, and it was perfect the way I wanted it.

But I'd wanted a Supra forever and ever and ever, and when I finally got it, for a minute I thought I was the coolest thing ever. But it was heavy; it didn't turn like I wanted it to; the turbo gave out after a few weeks; whenever I hit about 4,000 RPM on a takeoff, the fuel cut, and the turbo seized. It showed a disgusting lack of power. Even when the thing ran well, it didn't do what it was supposed to.

Theoretically, that Supra was ten or twenty or a hundred times better than the crappy little RX-7 that I loved. I put the Supra on a pedestal without understanding that just because it was more expensive and more iconic didn't mean it would never break down. I never thought it would suck going around the corner. I never thought I'd have to break the rear end free to pull a U-turn on a three-lane road. In short, that Supra was a pile of shit.

I always wanted a house, so I got a nice house, and I thought it was amazing and wonderful. It turns out I prefer living out of a backpack because having a house means I have all this crap to do that I didn't have to do before and all these bills I have to pay. I spend most of my time in three rooms of the house. I live in the kitchen, the living room, and the place where I sleep, which might be the kitchen and the living room, depending on a drinking night. Otherwise, sometimes I sleep in the bedroom.

When I got to be a CTO of a company that was valued somewhere around $30 million, I thought it would be amazing to own part of it. I thought being the owner, manager, and boss of a company would be the best thing that ever happened to me. But it turns out I hate managing people—I just hate it.

What I love is building my art. I love writing code, metalworking, woodworking, and pushing myself to 3D-print something cool. What I don't love is trying to explain to my employees why getting drunk and pissing all over the carpet at the client's Airbnb and then falling down the stairs at the airport with Pelican cases are not okay.

The entire time I'm talking to my employees about those scenarios, I want to laugh because on one level, I find them hilarious. I don't want to have to be the one to stifle a smile because it's bad for business to tell them otherwise; I want to be the dude sitting next to him drinking beer who asks, "Whoa! Did you get fired?"

I thought it would be cool to get a CEO job, but the reality is I hated it. Probably just because it was a small business, but whatever. Nothing is perfect; everything has caveats. The more money I've had, the more people stick their hands out to me. When I was a kid, my grandfather used to say that everybody's got their hands out, and you have to slap them away. I didn't believe him; I thought that when you get rich, life is perfect.

Nope, it gets worse. You spot the fake friends, the people that need something, the people that make you feel guilty because you're not helping them. By the end, you become this bitter asshat you didn't want to become. You always thought you were super nice, but you found out you're protecting yourself. And now you're shunning things that could be good as well because there's a high probability they won't be.

Everything is real, and these things will change you. Take the time to be true, see what's real, and understand what's comfortable for you. Maybe the CEO is a great job for you, but I wouldn't focus on anything but your reality at the moment. I wouldn't give up what's real today for something that's not real to you today: collect the real.

Luckily, I end up broke a lot, so that problem comes and goes.

Pussy on a pedestal.

It's a terrible saying, but it's hilarious: you create this image in your head about another person. You put that person on a pedestal, and suddenly, that person is no longer a real human being but an *object*. You forget that the person has human emotions or feelings. Even if you were to end up dating this person you put on a pedestal, there would still be good and bad times. It wouldn't be perfect; you wouldn't be dancing and frolicking through the daisies with her in a white dress and you in your '20s garb.

No, that doesn't happen—you end up in a real situation. You will have arguments. Somebody will get sick. Somebody has to go to the store. Maybe they're insane, and you didn't see that because you were busy perceiving the outside appearance.

Likewise, it's easy to forget that famous people are real. While they have lifestyles and these awesome cars you see on TV, you never think about their day-to-day lives. They wake up; they brush their teeth. Maybe they drank too much and had a hangover. They have to shower; they have gross bodily functions like the rest of us. We're all gross, disgusting animals, but we hide it well.

Heinz Prechter, a very successful man out of Detroit, shot himself in his pool house even though he had all the money one could dream about. He was still a person who felt alone and needed other people. Celebrities in any realm don't become magical beings. You might think it would be great to be them, but do realize they're real people too—with real human problems. They're not infinite, and they aren't superheroes.

It's the same with the poor, the trailer trash, or "those damn immigrants." You lump them together and forget they are real people too. They eat, they sleep, and they have valid feelings. We are equal.

The TV Star.

I've hung out with a well-known TV star at a three-day event in Nicaragua, and it was an interesting eye-opener for me. My company was providing internet custom apps for this event sponsored by a cell phone manufacturer. The party was held at an exclusive club, one of those Soho House-type things. A top-shelf alcohol company came together to put on this event for a bunch of rich people, one TV star, and forty or so influencers and club members.

(An influencer is a person with no actual talent on display, in case you were wondering.)

When I see the TV star, I think about his characters on TV. I see him partying with everybody and having this great time and think it must be nice to be the center of attention and everybody is doing everything to hang out with you and have fun. I don't even talk to the guy for the first two days, but then on the last night, my staff and I are exhausted and finished with what we had to do for the week. I sit down with a beer at the back of the infinity pool to watch the sunset overlooking the Pacific. I could see for miles, and it was one of the prettiest places I've ever been to.

As the sun goes down, the TV star sits down next to me with a beer and cheers me. "Fucking workdays, huh?" he says.

We laugh and get to chatting. These days are exhausting for him too, as this is work. He says he doesn't like that he has to keep going, but his job is to party until 4:00 a.m. He doesn't want to party until 4:00 a.m., though. He wants to watch the sunset, do morning yoga, and maybe have ten minutes alone to listen to the birds and the monkeys in the jungle. But he doesn't get that: partying is his job, and this is what he does for an extra living.

We have a long conversation about his time hanging out with his group of friends. We talk about the stars of the show he's worked on and the relationships and the dinners they had together. I never thought that these A-listers and B-listers get together and have dinner where somebody cooks at their house, just like the rest of us. They have conversations about what's going on in their lives, their struggles at work, and who they're dating. It's less of TMZ and more about real people doing real things. They get sick, they have rough times, they have great times, they have friends, and they have family. You forget this because you only see the TV lifestyle and the parties.

Don't put anybody on a pedestal. Not your favorite musician, artist, minister, president, or even your parents. Nobody should be on a pedestal. They're just people who have difficulties, and they lie, and they tell the truth. They're figuring it out day by day, just like you and me. It can feel like some of us are special snowflakes, but we're not. We're mathematically negligible, but it's also freeing once you understand how insignificant you are.

We're all going to live and die. We have nearly infinite social opportunities given our expiration date versus the number of people in existence, but we will never meet that many people. We can take some risks; we can lose some friends. That person you see as the biggest person ever, that minister, that person who runs the karate dojo, they're all not that big in the grand scheme of things. These people run a business, but they're one out of 200 million people doing the same thing—so why should any single person be on a pedestal for you?

Now, that's not to say they should be below you, but what it comes down to is that we are all equal, and if there is a difference, it's a difference in the environment or a difference in beliefs. But we should not feel small or large around anybody. Take some risks, who cares? Seven and a half billion people live on this planet, so do what makes you happy. There's no reason to feel bad about having shitty friends when there are so many other people.

Letting some people go is going to hurt for a second, but a little short-term pain for a long-term gain will help you realize that nobody is above or below you. It helps to keep that in mind. Remember that book *Everybody Poops*?

Nailed it.

III

Interpersonal Principles

Education

Family as early sources of education.

My father was a mechanical engineer who worked on cars in Detroit and helped design sunroofs. At one point, he was VP of a multibillion-dollar company, but he wanted a little less responsibility, so he moved back to being a director. He's now an executive in a tier-one automotive company. He loves cars and building, and early on, he taught me how to work with my hands and visualize forces to build things or solve problems. He taught me that anything in the world was playable, meaning I could build and break anything to learn. It was rad to learn from my dad that failure was okay in the process.

He quit his job when I was ten or eleven years old to become a youth minister at a church, which, frankly, the whole family hated. We were even poorer than before, and we blamed the church for our situation. I want that faith, and I do have faith in God, but as I explained earlier, I refuse to go to churches because of my earlier experiences.

After a year at the church, my mom said, "That's it—we're moving to Florida." We picked up and moved so she could work indirectly for NASA on the solid rocket boosters on the space shuttle. My dad couldn't find a job in Florida because he was an automotive mechanical engineer and had no big qualifications, so we moved back to Detroit so they could both work in the automotive industry—after the divorce.

My father didn't shine like my mother did, as she has five degrees and was always at the top of her class from electrical engineering to law to mathematics. We were poor seemingly because she was always working on a degree, and she's brilliant, but always focused on her career. I wouldn't call her cold, but her need to excel and drive to work rubbed off on us. I've always focused on career over people, which I've had trouble shaking.

My grandfather and grandmother on my dad's side, Gramps and Grams, were my favorite people in the entire world. I learned how to control and carry myself from them. Gram's mother was impressive too; she went to the hospital with a slipped disc at 103 years old after trying to remove a tree stump from her backyard with a hatchet. She died at 108 last year, on Christmas day. She was amazing, and I loved her and learned a lot from her, including how to be an adult.

Grams survived breast cancer twice and lived twelve years after a heart transplant. She focused on people and was an upstanding person with a knack for fashion and being classy. If I didn't know which way the soup spoon went or wore black socks and a brown belt, it was trouble.

Gramps was small in stature, but he was the epitome of what many consider to be a man. He was strong of heart, but he wasn't the smiling type; he'd mutter under his breath and swear. But when he smiled, I was so stoked. His focus wasn't on people, but on money and politics. But one might argue he was more focused on people than most, but with a higher-level view. He had a great career with one company after the military, and when he retired, he bought the tallest hill in the town of a thousand people he grew up in and built his mansion overlooking the town and the river in Missouri.

Although Gramps was an eccentric, and that was nice, he came across as rough. He didn't have many friends, but everybody loved him. He was the first person to use words to put you in your place, but also the first to use actions to lift you. He taught me to shoot when I was a city boy. He was too shaky in his older years to shoot the skunks, so he had to teach somebody else to do it. Unfortunately, that person was me.

Learn at the workplace.

I think college was a big waste of money for a piece of paper. You trudge through to the tune of crap that's cobbled together and handed to you in spoonfuls, all of which is pretty damn useless in the outside world. When you're doing things yourself, you get an education fast. My jobs have always been so much better to learn from than college because when you're working and doing your best, you never stop learning.

One way to continue to learn is to put yourself in positions where you're doing something you want to know how to do. In my world, for example, if I write the software, the next step will be to work on the circuit. Next, I could move on to some mechanicals, and then I can try to CAD up a design and make some 3D models.

You'll find two things happen when you're learning on the job. You're enjoying what you're doing, and other people are enjoying what you're doing. As you're drawing in more parts of the role, you end up putting on more hats and get better at your specified role too, because now you're understanding more of the surrounding architecture.

Positioning your job and going the extra mile at work is more for you than the surrounding people. It's not to get a better paycheck. Studies have shown that a better paycheck makes you excited for a little amount of time, but it doesn't help morale at all. To feel valued at work is to continue to learn. I've always started leaching my job into every other job that my position interfaces with. Then I can speak to the people around me better while I learn, which is the fun part of life for me.

Do random projects on your own time.

I have so many unfinished projects, because I don't think it matters if you finish everything as long as you're learning. The other day, I put a compass inside a clockface on wood, inside an antique toolbox with felt lining, and set it up with buttons. Doing the project, I learned how to refurbish better, and there's no reason to finish it, because where am I going to put that in my house? Nowhere. Who will buy it? Nobody. It's not mechanically sound, but I wasn't looking to get mechanically sound.

I was looking to understand how the wood interplays with the felt, the paint, and the rust. I wanted to know how to make clean pieces and dirty pieces come together. This was a thought experiment, and when doing these kinds of experiments, you don't have to finish them.

For example, I've built eight or nine motorcycles. I take them all the way down and put them back together in a different way with more parts with different configurations. I chop them down, rebuild them, and then give them away or sell them for some ridiculously low number. It's not about the result; it's about the learning journey.

YouTube is a double-edged sword.

Saying you watched it on YouTube and did it once does not make you a professional—we've all seen Pinterest fails. But you can absolutely use YouTube to incrementally move your skills forward. You won't build a robot by watching YouTube, but you can figure out how to drive a servo motor, which is a part of a robot. Eventually, you'll get to that robot.

I grew up with search engines, so I'm wired to know how to ask the right question. The key is not in the answers but in asking the right questions. You create a relationship with the search engine after a while so you know the right keywords to get an answer. If I'm writing software, I will probably do three hundred to five hundred queries to Google in a single day.

Once you know how to ask the right questions, finding things on YouTube isn't hard, but the trick is scope. When you're on YouTube, stay within your scope. Searching "I want to build a robot" means you won't get a bunch of crap on how robot knees work. I suggest you start in Google with "How do robot knees work" and read an article and look for the explicit terms, such as servo motors and bearings. Then enter those queries into YouTube, and perhaps ask "How do bearings work?" and "How does a servo motor work?" and so on. Then take what you learn and bring that back over to Google, look at the pictures, and start your learning process.

My suggestion is to go top-down and bottom-up. Starting at top-down is checking out the forest by going broad, such as "I want to build a robot." But you need to understand the roots of the trees to understand the forest. Jump back and forth from the details at the bottom to the overview at the top until you've got a clear picture. The middle usually becomes immediately visible when you see both sides.

Being scoped is important in learning. Make sure you're staying within a basic camp so you understand the terminology and won't be overwhelmed. Don't dive into quantum physics; drop a ball, see what happens, and eventually work your way in once you've got the physical world down.

Break things.

I often say nothing's sacred. For example, sometimes when building things, I'll get an object of great value (read: over $10,000) to take parts from or disassemble. Most people will be touchy about taking that stuff apart. I have no reverence; I take it apart and get into it. If it's been built, you can fix it or build it again.

Sometimes trash can be a great place to start. My buddy had a car he rolled over when I was in college and sold it to me for $100. I went to Home Depot and picked up a sledgehammer for $9, a piece of tubing for $12 for the exhaust, and flat black spray paint. This project was my favorite moment in education because it was the first big thing that I had no love for and could do whatever I wanted. I taped it off in the parking garage at college and spray-painted it. The police came over and asked, "What are you doing?"

I looked up and smiled. "I'm painting my car." At first, I thought I would get arrested or something, but the cop laughed and said, "Oh, we did that in college too."

That cool moment led me to understand that everybody is learning in that same way: by doing. In school, you learn the keywords, but they don't teach you how to think. They say, "Here's an equation."

"Oh, that's cool. What kind of equation?"

"Well, that's the kinematic equation."

"Why do I need it?"

"You need to memorize this, and then you use it for this problem in this way."

Whereas the reality of an equation is if you look at something, and you understand all the parts involved, you can build it by thinking. You'd have to be a super genius to come up with something out of the back of your brain, so you need some experience with it.

Consider physics. You look at a ball rolling down a hill and see gravity and inertia. Okay, cool. It's in the air, so there's fluid friction. You can go all day thinking about everything involved. Yet we're taught to memorize and apply. We have to memorize every situation and equation and hope that the two work together, such as the two trains departing from different places at different times. However, if one of them is a car, then what? Nobody taught you how to deal with one car and one train—they only taught you to measure when the trains would crash.

The biggest misconception we're given is that math is something we should memorize. Now history, we can memorize, but you still need to understand the template of history. We're so focused on memorizing and storing data when there is zero need for us to do so today: we need to store templates. If I need to know what date the War of 1812 began, I could probably guess it was somewhere in 1812, or I could just Google it.

What matters is realizing that mass genocide hasn't gone well for anybody. Nobody likes genocide. Cool. So don't do that. Hold on to that template, not the actual details. You can find all the details, so don't waste brain space to memorize them, learn the template.

The biggest template is that you need to explore or "explode" something before you can figure out how it works. Instead of looking at something as magic, take it apart and investigate all the little pieces. Almost everything in a system has a reason, so investigate and learn. Take it down to its tiniest pieces to understand it.

Take toothbrushing, for example. If you're just going to run this plastic across your teeth, you're not learning anything if you're not templating the activity. But if you're thinking that the beginning goal is how to get this crud off your teeth, there are a lot of ways you can do it. You can run a leather belt across your teeth. You can use your finger, or you can use a toothbrush. But why a toothbrush? Well, the bristles are small; they get in the cracks. Okay, that makes a little more sense. Now what's the point of the toothpaste?

Break things down into their components. Define the problem and the pieces in the system, and then look at the thing as a whole. Understand the details before you look at the whole, but don't get bogged in the details.

Don't become stale or compare yourselves to others.

Competition with others is a great tool for learning. You learn fast if you're competing with somebody. But how do you avoid comparing yourself if you're competing? Surely, that's the basis of competition.

It might be cocky, but I don't have anybody I aspire to be other than the best me. I dealt with this for a long time because it's similar to sports when you think that another guy is better than you, and you have to beat him. It's the same in engineering. But the reality is I only want to be the best version of myself. I can't be them, so there's no sense in trying.

Compare your results, but don't compare yourself. Just because you didn't make as good a cake as the other dude on TV doesn't mean you're not as good of a baker. It just means that your ganache probably wasn't good that day. You could have made a better ganache, or maybe if it was a carrot cake, you would have won. The comparison between the two makes little sense. Now, taking little pieces of what they do or ways that they work, that's not comparing—that's learning from them.

Learning comes from discomfort.

I was building a generator shed when I was learning woodworking, and I didn't understand what I was doing. I cluster-fucked my way through the tools, and there was one time I was using a scroll saw to cut a half inch off things. I had my fingers placed right, and I was getting it darn straight and moving it.

This desert rat from across the street in the middle of nowhere was hanging out with me. Our properties are on ten acres looking over a valley where they do music festivals in the desert. There's nobody around, and so this dirty dude covered in tattoos who had all his teeth replaced after meth destroyed them looks at me and says, "Give me the screwdriver or the drill."

He takes a long skinny piece of wood, plugs it up top, screws it in on both ends and says, "Now run your tool along that." And it was one of those moments where I knew you can learn from anybody. Just shut up and listen. This dirt ball showed me up in the biggest way in two seconds: zip and done.

See, an educated person today has no look. It doesn't matter what you look like, or what gender, age, or race you are. I've met people who surf all day, every day, and you talk to them and learn they're brilliant. I've had some of my best mathematical and quantum physics discussions while sitting in the middle of the jungle with a bunch of surfer bros smoking a joint. Everybody has the same propensity for learning, so, to circle back, learn from everyone you encounter.

I let my desert rat neighbor spend a few weeks at my house, and we spent one Christmas together. We get together, have barbecue, and hang out now and then. He's taken me on the craziest adventures off-roading to mines. This guy pushes me harder than anybody. He hops in his little four-by-four, and since he's been driving the desert forever, he takes me on the craziest paths.

The first time I drove my 1959 Willys Jeep off-road was when he took me to a place where I was looking over about a four-hundred-foot drop. The road has a *V* chunk out of it, and I ended up at about a ten to fifteen-degree angle going over. I had no idea how to drive this car, yet I had to do it. I had to get up in the mountains. I've never been so scared but so stoked in my life as to let this guy push me.

We were thinking about starting a show called *City Boy Survival* based on the situations he puts me in. For example, he'll say, "Here's an AR-15. Shoot that thing."

"But I've never shot an AR-15 before."

"You'll figure it out. Now here's a four-wheeler."

"But I haven't ridden a four-wheeler since I was ten years old."

"Great. Let's take this path. It's harder than the Jeep path."

Every time we go somewhere, he'll say, "You're the first person to be here. Not the first city person. You're the first person to be here in a vehicle like that—which is super cool."

To be fair, the Jeep's .327 under the hood and massive lift might've helped too.

He's educated, which is the crazy thing, and you wouldn't know by looking at him. He knows things that maybe you wouldn't think are important, or that you'd call dirty, but he knows a lot of useful stuff. Plus, the guy has more guns than anybody I know, so I'd best say nice things. Now I know how to use them too, and it was cool to learn while being put in a situation that made me slightly uncomfortable. When you're uncomfortable, you get scrappy, and you learn quickly because you have little choice.

Everyone is not equal, only born equal.

Our constitution says all men are created equal—but we are not equal. By that, I mean we all have the same chance at life, liberty, and the pursuit of happiness, but we aren't equal. And that's not to say that your looks, talents, and skills define your value. Your value is in your interpersonal skills, how you treat people and how you treat yourself when pushing yourself, driving yourself, and creating. If you have one person sitting on the couch eating Cheetos while another person strives to be the best person they can be, well, the two are not equal.

One is likely a drag on society, and the other is possibly pulling society forward. A janitor can clean to the best of their ability and set off a reaction for the people around them, and now they all have a high standard to emulate. It's not about your station in life; it's about your attitude and what you're doing and how you do it. The CEO and the janitor are equally important in a company. It might be easy to find a new janitor, but maybe it won't be easy to find a janitor who cleans the windowsills perfectly every time because he takes pride in having a clean space for the people he's helping.

Remember the saying about the weakest link? One total bummer will drag the whole team down because they demonstrate you can be half-assed and still get away with it. But if everybody's building each other up, that's huge. If everybody's respecting each other's position like they're the CEO of their position, then everybody and everything runs smoothly.

When I was twenty-two, I was in college, but I was a technical applications engineer without a degree. This company made a position for me after being an intern, which was cool. After my internship ended, I said I wanted to stay. Since they couldn't keep an intern that long, they offered to hire me to work thirty hours a week while I went to school full time.

It wasn't stressful because I never did homework; I negotiated with the teachers for a grade. Most of my classes were in electronics, so I'd show them what I was doing at work and say, "You're probably not going to teach me much in this class, so can I have a B and just not show up?"

That worked in a couple of my classes as I found that if I pushed the teacher, eventually, they would let me go. At work, I was making cars drive themselves on 129 core processors while at school, they were teaching us the simplest processor in existence. They'd say, "This is how an interrupt service routine works."

I'd say something like, "No, an ISR works this way: you have a prologue and epilogue to push and pop the stack, then the program counter is moved and must be returned..." I kept putting so much data out there that eventually the teacher isn't teaching the class and the kids are getting confused because I'm talking light-years ahead until the teacher would say, "Please stop." It was a tactic, probably not a good one, in retrospect.

I loved building stuff, but I didn't enjoy being at work. The big boss didn't like me, the head guy. We had a J-shaped office where it trailed off into five cubicles in a dark hallway that dead-ended. He put me in the second to last cubicle with no one within ten cubicles of me. I stuck out like a sore thumb. I had these earrings; I listened to metal; I was still nice to everybody and did everything I was told, but I just didn't fit in, even though I dressed well.

Find mentors.

George was this large, burly guy with a lot of freckles and the biggest smile you'd ever see. Every day, this lumberjack of a guy stuffed himself into a polo shirt and some khaki pants to come to the semiconductor manufacturing company where we both worked in the sales office. A whole lot of the things in this book I learned from George.

My job was to take brand-new chips, silicon microprocessors, and make demonstrations for them to use in sales presentations. I got to have the newest parts and build them into the coolest things, such as cars that drove themselves. In 2008, they tasked me with making RC cars drive themselves with a camera and a bunch of sensors and go around a track and pass each other. Today, not a big deal. In those days, it was huge. I even added a thing called Drunk Driver Assist— long before LDW warnings were a thing.

It was a cool spot to work, except it was awful because I was a young dude surrounded by dumpy, middle-aged people who had families but weren't stoked about it. We were going around one Monday morning talking about what we did over the weekend. Every week, the normal chat was, "Well, I cut my lawn and took the kids to soccer" or "I put up a new basketball hoop for the damn kids." You could see in their eyes they were dead in the middle of Michigan, northern Detroit suburbs, the middle-class hell. Where dead dreams go to die again.

One day, I wanted to see if I could mix things up a bit during our Monday morning catch-up time. We went around the table, and the guy before me said, "I worked on the house a bit, got things cleaned up nice."

Next, I said, "Yesterday morning, I woke up hungover in the back of my car in a casino parking lot with $300 in my pocket. I have no idea where it came from. I remember playing games, but I don't remember winning or passing out in the car."

Everyone stared at me. Afterward, George pulled me aside and said, "That was funny, but you can't tell people things like that. In the professional world, it's best to keep it to the boring stuff."

George became a huge mentor as he took me under his wing to teach me how to do the personal side of things. I could build anything, but I was a weirdo in a professional setting. It seemed odd, since I found all the other people weird and dead-eyed. They were the quintessential people I aspired not to be.

In the mornings, George would chat with me for five or ten minutes, and I'd try to understand the psychology of sales, which was his world. I wanted to know about psychology and how to work with people positively. How do you make a client feel good? How do you become a better salesman?

George could sell anything to anyone, and this guy's personality enthralled me: I wanted to learn why he was always so happy. It turns out he wasn't always happy, but he knew the key to getting to people and understanding them. He taught me the difference between listening and hearing: hearing is passive while listening is active.

One time, I was complaining to George about a gentleman I was working with: "This guy is just a jerk. He's messing everything up. He doesn't care. I think he hates me."

George said, "Did you know that you can learn something from everybody? Don't just write them off. Take the time to figure out what's alienating you from them."

I should have taken his advice when I was younger because a few things came out of that. If you're not learning from somebody, you're angry at them, and it festers. If you're watching them like they're in a zoo—by that, I mean there are bars between you and them—then you're both safe. Maybe you're not in the zoo, but if you split it up in that manner, then you can take the time to see what's driving you nuts and then not do that to drive other people nuts.

Everything we do is about relationships. While you can't afford to burn a single person in these technical worlds, you shouldn't burn a person, anyway. Most worlds seem a lot smaller, so I probably should have listened to George. His advice didn't sink in for another five or ten years.

The biggest thing I learned from George is that sales is not a game—it's relationship building. You aren't looking to put a product in anybody's hand; you're looking to create a relationship between you and the client and between product and client. That goes both ways: you want the right product for the right client. George's big advice was, "You don't sell somebody something they don't want or need— you sell them what they do want and need."

But you also sell yourself and your organization in a relationship manner. You don't fake it. Nothing he taught me was about faking. Of course, you put yourself in a jovial mood and all that to be outgoing. But beyond that, you're not telling people what they want to hear; you're telling them the truth.

Paul

When I was working for automotive as an engineer on super-cars, I did the architecture for gauge clusters. I supervised the team that would make sure all the other teams play nicely. We weren't their boss, but we were in charge of making sure everything worked together and was as close to perfect as possible. When you can't tell anybody what to do, you have to bump them back in line with logic. This certainly teaches you a lot of patience.

I worked with a gentleman named Paul, an older dude who smoked a lot of cigarettes. He was what you'd think of when you picture a stereotypical engineer: he wore a button-down, short-sleeved shirt with a grandpa pattern on it, and he always had a pack of Marlboros in his shirt pocket. I assume that's why he had to wear it, so he could keep his Marlboros somewhere. He looked professional, but he looked like he had been smoking forever. He was only around fifty years old. This guy had the grossest car, and he smelled disgusting, but he made a lot of money. He helped me to keep calm, as we were in a fast-paced environment, so he taught me to be an airplane.

"When you're flying an airplane," Paul said, "you don't adjust for the currents of the wind. You adjust for where you're going. You let it throw you, and you just re-aim at the end once you're done flinging around. You just gotta roll through and stay calm."

We worked together for about a year, and he took me under his wing during that time. Paul was one of those people who molded me in a big way and helped me get through my first true management role, where I was overseeing a reasonably large team and huge developments. He was my sounding board that helped support me as the manager of people more than twice my age with over ten times my experience. He talked me off the cliff every day while we smoked cigarettes out behind the office.

He molded me both by example and by talking it through. He always had an ear for me. He'd listen, we'd chat, he'd tell me how to manage people without being a boss. From him, I learned that you pull people instead of push people, much like religion. If you hit somebody with a Bible, they will run away from God. But if you have an awesome life, and they ask you why, and you tell them you have faith, then they might ask a few more questions.

In business, if you're telling people what to do, they'll keep asking why. But if you do a great job and pull them along, eventually, they'll realize you know your stuff. Their "why" isn't, "Why should I do that?" but rather "What's behind this so I can understand?" This changes the dynamic between a boss and a leader.

The biggest thing he taught me was how to be a leader instead of a boss. Being a boss means being a huge dick, but being a leader means that people want to gather around you. You're a snowball rolling down the hill, and people are hopping on like snowflakes, and together you become this massive force.

Paul made himself more approachable than other leaders in one way because he was jovial. He looked like the biggest greasy Detroit dirt ball you'd ever met, but he was always smiling, and you could see in his eyes he cared about people. The best leaders truly care about people. They might be there to become millionaires, but they're also there to lift everybody around them. They're not cutting people down; they're building them up. When you're building a pyramid out of people, you're not stepping on them, and you're not making a pile of bodies to stand on.

Paul took the time to make a "good news sandwich" when talking to people. He didn't say, "This part of what you're doing is broken. Fix it." Nope. Paul would say something akin to, "Great release! This part seems to interfere a bit, mind taking a look? I look forward to the updates." He was great at talking to people and respecting them as humans. He'd talk about the why of the situation and how you could better it, but also deliver the good news if you did okay. He always made it a conversation; it wasn't a talk down.

He'd ask, "How's your family?" That was always a great question to hear because it wasn't fake; he really cared to hear your answer. He had pictures of his family on his desk, which many people do, but he had such pride in his eyes when he talked about them.

He never grumbled about his wife. When his kid graduated from high school and got into college, he was so proud. If his daughter did the smallest piece of art or something like that, he would show me the picture. You could see the love in his eyes. It wasn't like most people who grumbled about having to go home to the wife and kids.

Paul was excited to do things with his family. He'd take them camping frequently, as he loved being outdoors in his happy place. He adored his wife, and if there was ever a time to pass away, I feel like he chose the right time because I've never heard a person so happy and ready to go out on a high note. He was jovial and happy when we were putting out around two million car gauge clusters in over a year and a half. The rest of us were running ragged and freaking out while Paul was stoked on his family.

One piece of advice I appreciated was to never take off Friday; take Monday off instead. When you take Friday off, you'll get emails all day, and people will wonder where you are when they're trying to close the week. Saturday will be okay. And Sunday you're back on emails, cleaning everything up for Monday. But if you take Monday off, then Saturday's all yours. Sunday, you're not cleaning up for Monday, and on Monday, people don't bother you until the end of the day. Do your cleaning on Monday night, and you get that whole weekend block. This advice was mind-blowing and changed my world.

I came into work one morning, and immediately, we were called into a meeting. When HR came in, they asked, "Okay, is everybody here?"

I said, "Paul's not here," and she just looked horrified. I knew immediately that Paul had died, and I had to walk out and go driving around for hours.

George taught me psychology and how to be a person, but Paul taught me how to navigate a professional environment. He was so influential on me, and his passing was shocking. I've seen many people disappear from my life in that way, but he and my grandmother were the two that hit me the most. They were the two people I respected, as they had the best interests of others in mind, and I was close to them at the time of their passing.

For a long time after Paul died, my work and life suffered. I drank heavily, and eventually, I had to quit the job because I couldn't stand to go to work every day and not see him there. Every time I walked past his cubicle, I was reminded of him.

I put a picture of him in the vehicle line he was working on and encoded and stored it in a space in memory with a clever name that nobody will think is a nonoperational code. His picture is *in* the last project that he put his heart and soul into. Now it's all over America and maybe around the world.

I've taken on a few mentees in my career.

My mentees were mostly de facto, as in somebody popped up, and we were ready. This past summer I mentored a young kid from Brooklyn, a nineteen-year-old with crazy dreadlocks. You'd immediately assume he was a gangbanger from the way he looked and spoke, but he wasn't.

I was on a job building interactions for a toy store when this kid comes up and says, "Yo, I want to know how to do what you're doing." He's a minimum-wage floor clerk who works at the store in the front, stocking shelves and selling.

I hear that a lot, so I say, "Okay, whatever."

He said, "Arduino is cool. I read about it online. I want to do that. In fact, I'm teaching myself to code right now."

Arduino is an open-source hardware and software company, project, and user community that designs and manufactures single-board microcontrollers and microcontroller kits for building digital devices. I had a bunch of little circuits and things to program in my road case, so I gave him an Arduino and said, "Here, do something cool with this and show it to me the next time I'm here."

I return three months later to do some updates, and I'm sitting in the back, and this kid sits down next to me. I've had this happen so many times before, so I'm thinking, *Here we go. I will have to look at his terrible crap and say nice things.*

He opens his computer and says, "Check out what I built."

It floored me. This kid had built the most beautiful web app, full authentication, full deployment to the cloud. It had maps tracking and database integration. The entire thing is what we call reactive, which means when you click something on the screen, it happens right away. There's no loading; the entire screen just realigns and does exactly what you want it to—seamlessly.

I worked with my company to get him a month's unpaid leave from their side and had him come stay with me at my house in the desert. He went to work with me every day, and for a month, we hung out and chatted, and I got to know the kid. I tried to give him everything I could about coding and building stuff because he was such a great coder.

I also tried to help him in how I'm hoping this book would help people, which is to provide a set of rules through experiences for the people we consider misfits. He went back to work at the toy store, and he's searching for a full-time job, but at the moment, he doesn't have enough experience. At least he has this internship, and he's going back to school.

I had to learn not to write people off because I'd gotten so jaded over time and started writing everybody off. I still hadn't taken George's advice to learn from everybody. A satellite engineer once said to me, "Listen, bud. Us smart people have a big problem with just writing everybody off because they're not as smart as us." And in this case, I had been ready to write this kid off, and that was wrong. This kid's probably smarter than I am; our brains are the currency in our world.

Perfection

We should target a 100-percent perfect product, life, and relationship while understanding that it can never be.

If you're a perfectionist, you'll go nowhere waiting for the perfect wave and never surfing; the trick is to make sure you surf with the right people. In engineering, nothing is 100 percent, yet we're trained in youth to do it right the first time. The reality is that you do it poorly the first time, then make it as nice as you can with iterations. There's always one wrinkle, and you can't get that wrinkle out, and even if you did, there will inevitably be something else that isn't right.

When you build a system, you can drive yourself insane trying to make sure every corner case, or rare but real case, is perfect. But every time you add a decision, you're only making it exponentially more confusing or difficult. In software, you often have "if this, then that?" which means one decision, two outcomes. Now, if for "this" and "that," you add another "if this and that" to each "this and that", you now have four outcomes. You keep going with this brutally simple example, and then you've got 8, 16, 32, 64, 128, 256, 512, 1,024, 2,048, 4,096, 8,192, and you can keep going on and on and on. By the time you're done with the software, you will have created hundreds of millions or billions or gazillions or paths.

Assuming you could ever make something perfect with a gazillion paths is reasonably impossible. So when you hear somebody complain about their iPhone, that's because they don't understand how complex it is to design and how many paths have worked well.

Now the funny thing is engineers tend to be perfectionists, so our inability to do perfect work drives us insane. That there are bugs out there no matter what we do is maddening to our profession. Perfectionism is the one thing we cannot attain, but it's the one thing we imagine feeling so good. There are water spots on my glasses, or there's dust on the windowsills: there's always something out of place. It feels like a bad thing, but imperfection forces us to get as close as we can to that perfection.

Just because you can't achieve something, doesn't mean it shouldn't be the target. We shouldn't target a 90-percent product or 90-percent life—we should target 100 percent. If you don't aim high, then you're not doing it right. Some people would tell you to be content with what you have, but I feel you should aim for the sky, and if you get a couple of feet off the ground, then be stoked that such thing happened.

Trial and error.

I try things out, which seems at odds with the principle of perfectionism but isn't. For example, if you marry your high school sweetheart, how are you to experience perfection when you don't know the difference between people? To understand the solution, you should fully understand the problem, so trial and error allows you to see different outcomes to seek perfection. A big part of trial and error is the vision, and that's changing your perception to understand the ideal of perfection.

For example, I went to India where I visited a new house built the year before. The corners were wiggly, the light switches were off-kilter, and the paint looked like shit. It was truly awful, but it was a big house, and I could tell that for the area, it was probably an amazing place. My brother-in-law works at Apple and lives in America. When I asked him about the house, he said, "For people out here, this is the best they've ever seen. Their vision is such that this house is perfect."

You know when you've seen your idea of perfection. But at the first blush of sin comes the indifference, which is much the same with vision. Once you've seen something a little more perfect than before, that becomes your new standard for perfection.

In understanding the target, the experience of failure is a great teacher. If you always make the same cake, it's the perfect cake for *that* cake, but it's not *the* perfect cake. When you marry trial and error, you find that target in your mind and make your way to the goal of perfection. Then you're on to find the next target.

Your client won't know what perfect is, but they have a conglomeration in their head of what they want to see. Their idea is perfect because it has no flaws and hasn't been created. When they sell their idea to you, you have no target. You know the function of what they're requesting, that they want it to be pretty and perhaps painted red. To get to perfect, trial and error is the path from the diamond in the rough.

The goal of the invention of the telephone was to allow you to talk to other people. But that sexy piece of equipment hanging on the wall with a rotary dial earpiece was something different from the original goal. A cup with two strings between them would satisfy the goal, but a beautiful Bell telephone satisfies the target and ups the level of perfection.

At my first real job, I supervised gauge cluster engineering where I developed a firmware platform. I ate, slept, used, and breathed this efficient, beautiful chip to its fullest potential. This firmware went into multiple supercar lines, and it's my proudest piece of work. It took me almost a year to write the code for my first gauge cluster. The second one took a few weeks, and the third one I had up and running primitively on the day they gave it to me.

Perfection drove me nuts. The prologues and epilogues of interrupt service routines were so wasteful I ended up rewriting them fully in assembly code—they were so inefficient I couldn't handle that lack of perfection. I ended up doing things my generation wasn't used to, and the prior generation would find usual. Web coders assume we have infinite memory, speed, and processors. For me, it was this world where I saved a few nanoseconds, and because of that, I'd see an overall return of 0.64 percent efficiency, and it was a game changer. I was truly happy living like that, but I haven't been happy since that architecture with my work because nobody has allowed me to take that time to create such beauty.

I've always been under more time pressure to finish things. But the scale that automotive works versus the scale that consumer startup hipster culture works is that automotive expects a bunch of dead-eyed people to work forty hours a week max. I had a year to do this thing, and for me, that was a lifetime versus the norm where they staff it, and we have six months to finish, assuming everybody's working eighty hours a week, which not only kills everybody but also kills the quality.

I miss the motor world. I don't like startups anymore, but I can't sit around and do nothing either. I tried retiring, but that was super boring. I need to build my dreams, and my dreams are perfection. It doesn't matter what I'm building, but I must have the time to make it the absolute best it could be.

Come in with the humility to learn the solution.

I walked into a rather desirable job way too cocky when I was young and got smacked down. I was being the idiot when I didn't have enough knowledge yet to have that ego. I've been on all sides of it in this industry, and I always make mistakes. My advice is to find people with nearly your same skill set or who are striving to be at or above your skill set, and then the egos rarely come into play.

I've worked with my buddy Stanley for years, and he's now a firmware manager for a rather large, recent startup company we all know and love (or hate). He said, "I hired you, and then you were my boss, and then I was your boss, and now you're my contractor. And in none of this did I ever feel there was ego or somebody talking down to somebody. And I miss working with you because everything was about the solution—it was never about us."

When skill imbalances come into play, it gets to be about the people. But Stanley put it beautifully: it's about the solution. It's not about *whose* solution—it's about the perfect solution that balances the team with skills and pride and ego.

Perfect is the enemy of good because you never see it.

If you're focusing on perfection, you'll only see the flaws. For example, we were hanging out with my friend's child, who is the cutest baby; I love this kid, yet I felt that the baby didn't smile at me enough. And that's where perfectionism arrives in unexpected places: I had a happy moment, and then it was ruined because I was focusing on perfection and felt that the baby didn't smile at me enough.

I can see a perfect room, yet I will go nuts if I spot a tiny stain. When I leave my house for a week and come home, I think that my place is beautiful. A day later, my perfectionism rears its ugly head, and I think, *This thing has to change. That has to change. Those blinds are dusty, and I don't want to clean them. Holy crap! This place sucks. It's the worst.* And within a week, I hate my house again.

That's a good reason why a perfectionist working in a company and not working for yourself can be helpful. As an employee, you have program managers to keep you in check. There are two camps: if it were up to the engineers, they would never release the product, and if it were up to the program managers, it would be released immediately.

I would work on my architecture my entire life and never put it in a car, so it requires an outside observer: they cannot allow me to run alone. Somebody has to keep me in check, or nothing of mine will ever hit the market. Starting is easy, but once I get into it, I see the twenty years it'll take to perfect it when all I need to see is the two weeks to get it to a good state.

That's where the client driving and the program manager driving come in because they provide an attainable, solid goal. I won't get overwhelmed by chasing perfection. I can't build my own product. I can build other people's because I know what their good is. The conundrum is that if I build my own product, and it has my name on it, it has to be perfect. Yet that's not possible.

Whoever said the customer is always right was definitely the customer.

Customers don't understand the world that we do. And generally, they have airs about them, and they can be condescending pricks. The customer generally has no clue what they want, and they have this, "Well, I have the money," thing. The funny thing is we have money, too, and we're taking your money. My first company's motto was, "The only thing better than spending money is spending a douchebag's money," because we ran into this kind of thing so often.

I have engineering clients, and they are the best to work with. They tell me exactly what they want, and they're grateful for the things we build, and so a big part of what I do now is to avoid clients who don't know what they're talking about. Ideas are cheap, and the money is usually from magic (daddy, investors, doesn't exist). I would rather work with people I want to work with to avoid that challenge.

You know they're good or bad at what they do. But I've noticed that if you can convince somebody to hire or partner with you in about thirty minutes, they'll likely be a terrible partner. If you see stars in their eyes when you start talking, they're likely not going to be a good partner for you.

I could talk circles around this firm in LA that did Interactive. Right away, they asked, "Can you build a better app?"

I said, "Yes, and it'll be this much money."

They said to do it; I didn't even have to sell. I wrote one silly app that wasn't even a silly app. They hired a guy they hadn't met who talked to them on one phone call to build this system that went into a bunch of malls. Frankly, I had written half an Android app in my life, and I just did this professional thing for a top cell phone manufacturer I sold on a phone call. It was mind-blowing, and they should not have hired me.

I should not have applied for that job, but I did it, and I succeeded because I knew I could; that's my cocky side. But I didn't take the time to learn who they were. They treated their employees terribly; they expected everything to be easy. They had no sympathy for me working long hours— and we're talking about nearly no sleep and never leaving the office and not taking holidays or weekends.

They saw the money, and when things were delivered, all they were focused on was the money and screwing people over. They got money, and they screwed people over, so I guess they succeeded. But that's not my jam, and I learned to make sure that my ethos aligns with workability.

This entire chapter ends on this point: don't be a dick.

If you're a perfectionist, learn to trust somebody else's judgment, because as a perfectionist, you will always think something will fail. It might, but it probably won't fail just because it's not perfect. Once I was at a big table of engineers who were delighted over being with Steve Sanghi, the CEO of Microchip Semiconductors for a dinner. Yet here I am, this cocky little kid with earrings, who looks at this CEO of a multibillion-dollar company and asks, "Why do your products suck?"

The table went silent. He said, "My original products suck. But I got them in your hands, didn't I? And my following product lines are even better than some of the best."

He talked to me about Hondas being known as the shittiest cars in the world when they came out. Everybody hated them, but they were cheap, and the kids could afford them. Later, when Honda was of better quality, those same people bought them again in their twenties and again in their thirties, and now Hondas are some of the best cars out there.

He said, "I saw Honda's business model. I saw a fab for sale. I only came up with $10 million to buy a semiconductor company, and you used my semiconductors in college. That meant that when you went into industry, you wanted to see if there was one of my semiconductors you could still use. So I gave you a subpar product, and then I gave you good ones. It's up to you to pick which applies to what you're doing. I never deprecated a product. The same parts you would've gotten in the '90s, you will get today. I never took one away from you."

I thought that was cool: it's not about perfection; it's about delivering.

Another point is to learn what not to do. Don't tell people you're a genius; never bring that word to the table. For example, there was this gentleman in his sixties who was interviewed to design satellite power supplies at a startup of all twenty-somethings. The guy was a brilliant hardware guy, but in his interview, he said, "You need me because I'm a genius."

He got the job and worked with us for a while; he made sure to always tell us how smart he was. He had long, greasy, gross hair. He never wore deodorant and smelled like the end of the world. He alienated everybody, and he could not do basic things like starting his MacBook Air. He was unable to Google even the simplest things. Had he brought humility to the table, I think we'd all have helped him happily. But what I learned is that it doesn't matter what your IQ is or how smart you think you are, keep it to yourself because it puts you under a microscope.

Don't talk yourself up; just talk about the project. Otherwise, everybody's looking at the fact that you can't boot up a MacBook. Don't tell everybody you're the best because then nobody wants to help you; they want to laugh at you. Let other people say you're smart. Don't be the one to tell them.

Ignoramus

That's me: I'm an idiot, a hypocrite. I repeat mistakes, but don't we all? People will tell you that they're different, but we're all the same. For example, I'm a liar. I don't mean to be, and I try to tell the truth, but sometimes I see things wrong and screw it up. Sometimes I tell a lie when I don't mean to do so, then I have to clean it up.

You keep doing the same things until you suck it up and say you're an idiot, but here's what you're doing right, and the next time, you won't do it that way. My advice is to go slow and take the time to do it right. Don't run a race, as nothing should be a race except with yourself.

Lesson: redux.

One of the biggest lessons in my life was seven years in the making. I have this acquaintance we will call Brad who treated me like a friend, but he only reached out when he needed me. He was the CEO of a few companies. He's the founder of one company you've definitely heard about, and you probably own some of his products. He has also another company that known in parts of the country. Now he has a third company that's doing pretty well, and he was also the CMO of a big internet company.

His venture capitalists kicked him out of his first company. The board callously removed him, and then he started another thing and came up with a $300-million valuation. He got $100 million from an energy company, and then he was removed again. Recently, we've been working on this project for the past year, and I felt terrible about my work product. I look back at everything that has happened and realized he was always racing to the finish line.

There was never a time when it wasn't a fire drill, so the quality was terrible. I put products on the market for him six years ago that were generally rated one-and-a-half stars on Amazon. "Why the f@#$ is this on Amazon?" was an actual review. They were dumb, rushed products, and we were proud of the fact we finished them superfast and did the impossible. I've been proud of it multiple times, but I'm left with this sinking feeling at the end that I haven't ever made anything of quality with this guy. It's always been trash because of pride in speed, not pride of product or engineering.

I've always looked up to him because I thought he was a great guy. He's boisterous; he's good at starting companies, getting people on board, and motivating people. Yet I missed this thing—the *what not* to do—which is not to sacrifice who I am or my quality and expect people to be proud I did it quickly.

This is huge because I'm seeing other suppliers get messed up in the head. A lot of us are feeling terrible and beaten down because this guy was a jerk to us when we failed. But he was the one who repeatedly put us in these terrible situations, and we were so high on the wins we didn't notice we were doing crap work.

We did great work for a five-day turn, but it should have been a three-month project, so you only see the crap at the end. Here I've made a huge shift. I don't want to race toward the finish line to get the money as fast as possible: I want to take my time and be proud at the finish line.

I'm tired of shortcuts.

I respected Brad for a long time, so that's been a shift too. I don't look at him and wonder what I can do not to become him. Instead, I ask, "What can I do to avoid his failings that give me a bitter feeling toward him?" I feel bitter about the poor quality of my product, yet I allowed him to put me in this situation. When I was close to it, I was mad at him. And when I pulled out, I was mad at myself because I could have said no at any point; he will do what he does. I needed to learn from that and get out of there.

You want Brad to like you, and I've heard this from many people I've worked with who have worked with him. You want his approval because all he does is use people. If you're one of the 10 percent he likes, then you're special because he's nice to you. He segregates everybody into groups, so he's got decoys, people that you can crap on so that the people that do well or have value are so much more excited they're not getting crapped on. With him, I feel small, and I don't know why, because he's the only person in my life that leaves me feeling that way and wanting his approval. Around him, I feel like a beginner engineer again, and I didn't know why.

I don't know why I care about him. But his personality is so Machiavellian that when you're close, you want to be in the light. If Paul had to separate you from the light, he was sad to do so. Brad used to walk around the office on a Friday and put his fingers like a gun to the back of people's heads and do the bang thing when they weren't looking—and you wouldn't see that person on Monday.

Paul would let nobody else know if something was wrong with you. He would talk to you privately if you had to be separated; he wouldn't tell other people about it. He helped me become better at firing when he said, "Don't tell anybody what happened. Getting rid of people should never be callous. It's okay to go to your car and cry after you've fired somebody because you have hurt their world even if they suck. It doesn't matter because they're still a human."

That was the difference between Paul and Brad. To Brad, we are all Legos, and if you lose a Lego, you can just get a new one. To Paul, we were all people. You can get a different one, but you'd never get *that one*, so he treated everybody like they were unique. It's love versus callousness—one person chases money and the other chases community.

Brad has always been abusive. But when you're a part of the in-crowd, it feels amazing, and they take care of you. But the second you're out, you're not a cool kid anymore, and they demolish you. But then you want to be back in, which is the hard part. You want to be back in those social graces again because you wonder why you're not cool anymore.

How you combat that feeling is to GTFO. Take some hits and separate, because if you don't separate, then you can't see how ridiculous you're being. You're feeling like you're in high school over money when you can go to a place like Microsoft and make money and be happy, fulfilled, and appreciated at the same time.

It seems like the shittiest, most mediocre people are the most successful because all they want is money. Whatever you focus on, you're likely to find in an economy like ours. But you don't have to want money. If you chase money, and money isn't your love, then you will not like your job; you will hate it.

To be happy, figure out what you're after. For me, it's perfection, the build. I want to be proud of what I build. I don't want to be a millionaire, so why would I mess around with people I don't like in situations I don't like to be a millionaire (which I also don't like but don't hate)?

Buying another car doesn't excite me anymore. In fact, there's little that excites me other than being proud of what I've done. You miss the positives if everybody around you is scrambling and fighting for money while building trash, and your skills or your drive are such that you want to be building something perfect.

But I was an ignoramus and kept hoping for a long time I could stay and make a go with Brad. When you're around people with low skill mixed with hubris—but they have money, slower skills, and a much bigger ego—that will drive you up the wall. That was Brad, who had all the cockiness and none of the technical skills, and was an asshole because of it. People skills are real, though, even if not in the positive sense we usually mean. Look at Edison.

It took me a long time to realize that the reason he was an asshole was that he was insecure, like all of us. It was a coping mechanism that worked in business. I still love the dude, but have lost all respect for him, which means next to nothing, in all reality. I wish him the best going forward. We all knew that he didn't know what he was doing and these products sucked. But it seemed like he was being an asshole just because he thought he was the best in that situation.

Brevity

No need for a lot of detail. Just the right details.

IV

Engineering Principles

The engineering principles of speed, quality, and price are constants in every industry.

My dad always told me to pick my two favorites between speed, quality, and price because you can't have all three. You can get something fast and expensive or fast at a low price, but it will be of low quality. You can get something fast and high quality, but it'll be at a very high price. If you apply this to your life, you won't be so pissed off that things didn't go the way you wanted because you got two-thirds of what you wanted: accept that you'll never get 100 percent.

I've learned that these stats are more akin to video game character stats. You have a total of two out of three of the things, but you can split it down however you'd like (i.e., two-thirds faster, two-thirds the price, two-thirds the quality). Nonetheless, you must find the balance appropriate to your product or appropriate to your situation.

I can call speed, quality, and price "engineering principles," but they apply in every industry, life, and situation you will ever deal with. It's the same in every situation across the world.

You want to build a house? You'll balance speed, quality, and price.

You want to have a successful relationship? You'll deal with speed, quality, and price once again.

You want the fastest, cheapest boyfriend? You're always going to get a low-quality boyfriend.

Keep these three principles in mind, and you'll understand why things happen. For instance, I have one client right now who wants to open a brand-new store in two weeks, and things keep failing and going wrong, and he keeps saying it's because the suppliers suck.

Well, no, the suppliers don't suck. It's that they don't want to spend the money to give them time, which means the quality suffers. Remember, you only get to pick two. You can pay a lot and allow a lot of time for quality. But if you're skimping, and you expect all three to happen, you're delusional.

There are other engineering principles, such as testability, maintainability, integrity, ethics, and management, but they are pedantic textbook behavior and principles. All those are important such as the integration to the world, the testability of the management, and so on, but those principles are where your head should be more trained.

More important than those qualities is your heart. If you're product-focused, and you love the product, all those principles make sense. If I were aiming to write an engineering book, I would focus a lot on those. But I want to focus on the heart aspects of things and the way things can apply across life, but they're a bit esoteric.

Speed

Don't go too fast and burn out; that boring stuff you feel compelled to overlook is very important. The reason I'm not sitting in a mansion right now—and instead have only four bedrooms and a guesthouse—is because I didn't watch my contracts, and I got screwed out of millions of dollars.

I went too fast because I thought contracts were boring. I trusted the people I was in business with, which goes back to my belief that everybody's a liar—so trust nobody. Even your mom could screw you over at some point; she might not mean to, but if she's looking out for her best interest, it could happen.

Politics versus speed.

Politics has been the biggest problem I've run into throughout my career. All I want to do is build cool shit, but I continually run up against the politics of speed. That's why this book is littered with examples of political nightmares.

It's hard to give timing on an engineering problem because you don't know what you don't know, but after a while, you get a good feel for it and how far it will go and what the work-arounds look like. That becomes manageable, but the people outside don't understand experientially; they don't know what you know. Teams outside of engineering are often volatile and emotional when it comes to the technical side.

When you're solely focused on the product, you tend to forget that people undermine people, that people get their feelings hurt when they're not as pedantic as you are. I worked with three great engineers in my career, and we would all argue and tell each other our ideas were dumb during the workday. Afterward, we'd get drinks and laugh and joke. We'd talk about totally different things or the product or laugh about something one of us said to the other. But when you have project management in the room, and they feel insecure about not knowing what you're saying, they'll possibly get hurt.

Don't worry, that goes both ways. There's always something that puts all of us off. I'm no different. Neither are you.

If your manager is not on a technical par with you, he's going to feel insignificant. He may not realize he has to lead you, not control you. I have had many managers with whom I get in tiffs because they're trying to assert control over something they don't understand. I can be hardheaded because I understand the problem inside and out, and when they try to assert their dominance or alpha status, it's *no bueno*. But there are ways to lead people smarter than you. Believe me, that happens to me constantly too. The trick is to set a target and listen to their ideas. Talk them through, and you'll usually find something brilliant.

I've never believed in hierarchy outside of merit, but the world at large sure does. The biggest issue I've had in my world is trying to explain to clients, to management—who are also clients—and to all the people around why we do what we do, what the timing is, and what the realities are. It just doesn't seem to go well.

I had a project that was a control panel for a mock-electric train for kids to go in and play and twiddle switches and do all kinds of fun stuff. Three pieces had to come together and make whooshing noises and beeps and boops, plus gauges to go up and down. I said it would take six weeks and cost about $15,000 to build. With the other projects in the build, it worked out to be around a six-figure job. That in conjunction with another larger project would have put us in operating range for the summer.

"Don't do anything right now," the client said. "We'll need you very soon, and you'll be very busy. Clear your summer"

So I waited, waited, and waited. I said, "Hey, my team's idle. I need to start taking other projects." Any time I tried to get out of the thing, they gave me soft approval but never a full one. The other project just fell off a few weeks later. Finally, I had to lay off my engineering team because I couldn't pay them. It's a small company and a small team so we can run on small bits, but we can't run with nothing coming in as these guys are expensive. Banking on two big projects at people's words was my mistake, no one else's.

About a week after I laid off the last guy, the client said, "Okay, we need the train now."

I said, "Great. So I have six weeks to build?"

"No, we need it shipped in five days."

Remember to smile. "It's not going to be high-quality, and that's really fast, so I need to charge you a rush fee."

"We're not paying a penny more, and we need it next week."

"It's going to be pretty low quality then. It's not going to be my best work."

But they give the okay, and I ask for all the information, get the outlines, and cut them on the laser. Along the way, I send them pictures, and they say it looks great.

Engineering principles: speed, quality, and time. You can only pick two.

I spend the time. I don't sleep. I do some of my best work yet. I buy automotive gauges, take the time to create a system to drive them as a car would function, so they go up and down, and you see the numbers for the temperature and pressure. We get a big, nice slider for a throttle, so it goes *vooom* like a real Eurorail, and we make it louder and quieter as you move the lever up and down.

We make a rumbling noise that sits underneath a bunch of random beeps and boops. There were probably fifty buttons across this thing. It's a beautiful, vibrant blue with bright-yellow accents. I etch their logo behind this clear acrylic, and everything is back-painted, so it looks like it's got a 3D depth to it. It feels fun, and you can't scratch it, because all the paint is on the backside.

It's some of my best work, but make no mistake, it's rushed. I ship it out and feel proud of it. I finally sleep a full night. When I wake up the next morning, the fab shop calls to say, "All the train panels are upside down."

I call the client, and I just lose it. "You approved this all along the way, you did not give me the time to do it right, I put my heart and soul into this thing. You weren't even willing to pay more! What's wrong with you? You treat all your suppliers like shit. I talked to two other people that you ran the summer out, and they lost tens of thousands of dollars from you, and you couldn't even look at the photos I sent you along the way and make sure they were correct?"

I lost my mind and fired that client. I got a call from their CEO who asked, "What's going on with you? We've known each other for years, and your quality is shit now?"

I tried to explain what happened, but he didn't understand. They're used to building furniture and putting fun things into places. They don't understand the difficulty that goes into my world, and I could not explain to them what it was, and no matter how many times I said, "This is going to be shit," they couldn't wrap their head around what that meant.

So they installed it wrong, and it broke on the first day. After being installed upside down, I put a fix in so it would make sense, and we made it work. However, on the first day, the front of this acrylic piece cracked because they hadn't put the under supports in—because they didn't read the three-page document I sent them instructing them to do so.

I won't work with that client again. I was so sick overworking I could barely stand, yet I still worked eight to sixteen-hour days. But I wasn't smiling. They were just assholes to me, so we're done. The biggest challenge is that they don't understand my world.

Quality

Just like in my previous story, to create something of good quality means not accepting projects you can't do well. The client doesn't know what they want, and this goes across all areas of life. When a client asks you for something, they don't know what they want. As an expert, you need to know what they want. The client will have this weird, fuzzy image of perfection. The client is rarely right because they don't understand what you do: if they were right, they would do your job. Conversely, the client knows the end-product requirements better than you ever could, so listen—and listen well.

Never underestimate how far shitty things can go.

After leaving the biggest tech company "ever," where I was working on firmware architectures toward perfection and spending the time to document and do everything right, I take a job where the owner is an ex-phone store assistant manager. He's a complete asshole whom I feel isn't good at anything. I lose it constantly because I say that we have to do this right; we have to do this perfectly; this is not okay. The way we're doing things makes little sense, and I'm running myself ragged because we're so far from perfection.

Yet based on things outside of perfection, we continue to grow. I'm losing my mind, and when I say never underestimate how far shitty things can go, I thought we would go out of business any day because this guy is yelling at everybody all the time. He decides he's a graphic designer, yet he puts the worst designs I've ever seen. It makes us look terrible, and my name is attached to this shitshow. I code out the ugliest UIs and hate them the whole time knowing I'll work my face off, build something beautiful, yet it will be ugly on the surface.

For lack of a better way to put it, it looks like a three-year-old with crayons designed the thing. It looks like I created UIs in PowerPoint. Dan keeps passing these designs to me, and I say, "Dan, this is terrible."

"Then you do better."

"I will."

"Well, you don't have time to do better. This is mine, and this is what the customer approved."

Dan gets mad at me because I offer other designs, and whenever we both put a design in, the client picks mine, and that upsets Dan. He stops allowing me to put designs in because he gets butthurt when his designs aren't chosen. Instead of placing emphasis on the company being better, he insists that his design be used. It goes so far that I finally say, "Fine, if you don't want me, hire a fucking graphic designer: if this is about you and me, then get a graphic designer."

Dan has never done graphic design before this point because he's a CEO, not a designer. He tells us this all the time, and whenever somebody questions his design and says, "Hey, I'm not sure that's the best way to do this," he immediately turns in anger and says, "I am the CEO of this company."

I'm the CTO, so the other business partner, the CFO, and I say, "We know your title." None of us really have titles; they're just paper designations.

When I started, we were doing about $1.2 million a year in revenue. In the end, we were doing over $5 million a year. Now they have about twenty employees, and they're still going. But in my head, I was sure they would fail because they sucked so badly at what they did. But they didn't fail because Dan scared all the employees into thinking they were worthless and couldn't go anywhere else, so he paid them less than minimum wage when he could. He broke people down and whipped them into staying, including me.

By the end, I was so beaten up. I hadn't slept in forever. I was working sixteen hours a day every day. I hadn't seen my family in eight months; I ruined relationships. Everyone at the company fell into the same trap. Yet this was Dan's way of making the company work.

Dan embezzled. He would buy a new TV for the company, bring his TV in, and take the new one home. He did the same with vacuums. He took rolls of paper towels home. It almost seemed he based his entire world on taking what he could from the company. We also did a lot of shady things to make things happen.

I saw $14,000 bills run up at the club when he would take so-and-so out from this big company. Why would you do that? That's not how this works. When I'd bring it up to him, he'd say, "Do you like being in business? Because that's how it happens." He'd take them out to the nicest club in LA or Park City or wherever they were with the client. I don't know how you spend fourteen or eighteen grand in one night at the club, but I know it involves cocaine. Don't worry, I also like cocaine.

To me, if you're not doing it right, if this isn't perfect, if you're not striving for perfection, you will fail. But they didn't fail. In fact, they're growing, and they're huge. They've expanded their business, and they're moving on to other clients. They've got shoe companies, internet giants, etc., and they're getting bigger, bigger, and bigger. I still talk to my developers, and they want to leave, but they don't feel they can do any better anywhere else.

It was the most incompetent team with the worst products I've ever seen, and I was part of the incompetent team because I allowed it to happen. They would tell me, "You have two days to make this product." I would say I needed three weeks. They'd say the product was already sold, and I had to build it in two days.

My incompetence in the case was that I couldn't say no. Many of these companies where I see the most incompetent people doing the worst things still keep going. Some of them fail, some don't. You can't go, "These people are incompetent, their product sucks. They will fail."

That's no guarantee.

And the people that drive these things have laser focus; they know what they want, and they do it. I've often villainized these people, but the reality is that they are assessing and using the opportunities provided to their fullest. Pyramids without slave labor are duplexes. I just don't have the heart for it. Thanks, Ray Kroc, thanks.

Price

If you want to build something cool, then don't take low prices. It's better to sit at home rather than lose money even if you want to build the thing. You're lying to yourself if you believe otherwise. You're setting a standard, and the next time you go to work with a company, they'll lowball you and say, "Well, the last time you did the job for four hundred dollars."

"The last time was an intro price."

"Oh, okay, then we'll find somebody else. It's chill."

They'll come back to you sometimes. But for the most part, you set a standard, and it's a stupid thing to do. Don't build something for a client for little money just because you want to—go home and build it for yourself.

At my first company, by the time I was done building motorcycle electronics and taking photoshoots with Miss America whilst her kid was running around, I was out of money and ended up having to move out of the place I lived in.

I crashed at my mom's house for a couple of months, and then I lived on my best friend's couch for another three to four months until I got a call from a German electronics company for automotive. They said, "Hey, we saw you when you were an automotive intern giving a presentation. We want to hire you," and I, being the cocky little asshole I was, said, "Okay. Fifty dollars an hour."

I show up, and they say, "Here's your offer for forty-two dollars and eighty-one cents an hour." I push it back at them and say something to the effect of, "No, I'm good sleeping on a couch unless it's fifty dollars an hour."

I got a call saying they accepted me for the job, and I was to have a drug test the next Tuesday. It was Friday when they offered me the job, and I was stoned out of my mind. So I drink water and exercise all weekend. I read about how they do the drug test, and on the initial inspection, they want to make sure the urine is a little yellow so it doesn't look diluted. I knew that B vitamins would turn my urine yellow, so I drank as much water as I could in the morning, and then right before the test, I downed a Monster energy drink so I would pass, after a long weekend on the '80s ski machine in the basement.

I went to a Catholic church to pray first, and I said, "I'm joining the Air Force if this doesn't work, God." I'd never been to a Catholic church except with my buddy as a kid, but I thought it was prettier, and if you had to talk to somebody about the future, that was the time.

That was the day I didn't join the Air Force and became an automotive engineer. My second company was where I had that moral issue with the project I was doing. I lost everything, sold what I had left, hopped in my car, drove for five months, and lived on about $1,200 after a bad casino binge. Those are the fun times. The crappy times are when you have money because then you're just plain bored.

In the end, I could've been flying fighter planes. Bummer I didn't fail that test, eh?

Learning

The point of this entire book is to advise you to keep learning. If you go about it the right way, you should be able to find a way to learn all the time, from everyone you know, from every experience you encounter. You should learn at work, at home, and out in the world. Learn the high level first. Understand the problem; only then will the details make sense. Stay out of the real world, stay out of the details (yet don't forget them), and then you can solve problems. But don't fool yourself: learning will be a continual process, not instantaneous.

The creative process.

Let's say somebody asks you for something, but they don't know what it is, and you don't know what it is because it doesn't exist yet. You only know what function you want and that it will be a reflection of you, so you want it to be sexy.

Daydream.

Sit down somewhere pretty or somewhere not pretty, close your eyes, and start drawing the product in your head. Start playing with the product. It's this mushy cloud of vapor at first, so think about what it is and start applying things you've seen.

What was the favorite charging method you've ever used? What was your favorite button? What was your favorite screen? What doesn't exist that *could* exist? What technologies have you seen that have blown your mind that you could apply? Things like on the MacBook Air, the LED you couldn't see where it was when it was off because they used tiny, tiny holes. How could you apply that to creating a screen so you can't see where the numbers are until they light through?

Start with this nebulous cloud of a daydream when making the perfect product. That's the first step. Many go right into the requirements, such as what it should look like or how it should work, but I recommend you start by playing with it. It's art, after all, so use your imagination. If you don't need this thing, then it's a fun project, even if you're doing it for money. That's the biggest part of the process. I always start sketching, doodling, and drawing, trying to make a fun page in a notebook. Because it's your product, your baby, it should be art from the beginning.

Following that, get pedantic, which is the part everybody likes: sitting in meetings and talking about the product. Unless you're creating an industrial design chair, and your function is to sit in it, you need to start with the functionality because that drives everything else. Even that chair may need this level of love. Probably does, what do I know? What does this do and how? You can have qualifiable things, such as you should be able to sit comfortably. But you want to target something quantifiable, such as 80 percent of people should be able to sit comfortably in this chair for at least twenty minutes.

A funny thing they teach in industrial design school is that the chairs at McDonald's are designed to become uncomfortable in twenty to thirty minutes. They want the customer out so the next customer can come in. Before this, though, that customer should enjoy their meal, so it should be comfortable. That's their quantifiable metric.

Following the functional definition, you can get into industrial design. If you get into it any earlier, you will end up having to throw a lot of things away, if you try to make it pretty before it's a thing. Parallel to the industrial design, you can start the engineering part. Then the engineers and designers can go back and forth, and the engineers can say, "We're gonna need two inches by two inches of circuit board space somewhere."

The industrial designer can say, "Cool. Can it be round or octagon? What can it look like?"

The engineer says, "Well, that's an interesting shape. Let's see. Here are my big components. If you lay the big processor or capacitor out, I can fit it and all my other little stuff in, so I'll worry about it later."

They go back and forth, and the designer's brain starts to get excited about all these pieces handed over to him, and he can ask questions such as "Can I make it glow here?"

The engineer can say, "No, that's stupid."

The manager can come in and say, "Yes, it has to glow."

When the requirements have been set, you start to define the product. Everybody has their little piece defined or sketched out—kind of a block diagram which is somewhere between the requirements phase and the actual development phase is in this design—like drawing block diagrams of processor, screen, battery, etc.

Once you settle on this nebulous blob of product, you know what you're targeting. You've got sketches from the designer and blocks from the engineers and software ideas from the software guys, and then you can start the development phase, which is where things get locked down.

The engineer says, "This is how much space you have."

The industrial designer goes to the mechanical engineer and says, "Here's how it looks. Don't mess with it more than two millimeters in any direction. Anything you change on the face, let me know." That's where the industrial designer starts dealing with finishes, colors, and that sort of fluffy, important crap, which is actually important. There are people whose job is to know which color will be in vogue the next year, and it's important because it helps sell the products.

The engineers need to lock down their products, make sure everything is set, and get to an initial prototype or the plan for an initial prototype, and then you start getting marketing involved at that point because it starts to turn into a product.

For the development phase, you start with prototyping, and you create one of your magic "thing," which is a pile of crap but looks and works a lot like what it will be. You avoid the big tests, and you can only make one, and it might only work for an hour instead of three years, but it validates the concept and allows you to see what breaks and so on.

The engineering side will often get a jump and make what's called a pizza box. That one won't even fit in the final product. Sometimes it will be as big as a, well, pizza box for the circuit board, and it allows you to test all the electronics and the software. The mechanical side will start doing 3D prints now. Back in the day, they just had to try to make it as perfect as possible, make a clay model by hand or send it to a machine shop where they would use a mill and calipers (and lots of other cool stuff) and create a prototype that cost a lot before the 3D printer came.

Everybody does their prototypes to see what breaks and what doesn't. Mechanical guys are dropping their things on the floor to see what snaps off, for example. Development becomes this delicate dance between everybody trying to get their thing perfect and integrated to everybody else's thing while negotiating in the middle. In the meantime, the investors must be satisfied with the progress, as well as leaders and sales. So a prototype helps let everyone show progress from their field.

There are lots of egos in play, so this is where it's key to be a leader—not a boss, not hierarchical, because the people in charge of making it successful are generally the people on the ground who see every piece and how all comes together. You need to think about everything as a holistic product. A lot of people are concerned with their one little piece, but it has nothing to do with the one piece. If everybody's looking at the product as a whole, you have great conversations.

Moreover, the leader doesn't have to be one person all the time. Depending on the activity, the group leader is the person with the most experience or acuity at a certain function. It is a role to be taken by the person the group deems most capable to direct the team to success at that moment.

Now you should have a focus; for example, mine was generally firmware, architectures, and circuits, but my understanding of the mechanical side meant I understood that the circuit board needed to fit in the mechanical, and I could give a hand to the other side because I have a brain too. So do they, and they often helped on my side.

A difficult engineering problem I solved (title written in crayon).

I worked on the gauge cluster for an American supercar when they brought it back in the last decade. We had a screen on it, a seven-inch TFT LCD (thin-film transistor liquid-crystal display). First, we prototyped it by using one of those picture frames I found at OfficeMax (if you kids remember that place) or one of those companies probably going out of business, soon—or already have.

We got a digital picture frame and soldered fifty-four tiny wires one by one to the product screen and then loaded that picture frame circuit board with all the images for what the gauge cluster should look like and showed it to Chrysler. They loved it. I had the biggest "noner"—that's a nerd boner—for months about that.

They 3D-printed the carriage for the screen and stepper motors (the things that moved the gauges), and they sent us this 3D-printed thing and said, "Make us a working gauge cluster," and it was up to me to make it work. I told my boss I didn't have time to do this during my day job. I asked him to hire my side hustle, my small company, to do this, which he did. My day job paid us to build a prototype to sell a project to a car company, which was awesome.

The biggest problem ended up later in production. We put the screen into the production hardware, and we got brand-new fresh circuit boards back. They were beautiful, and everything worked—mostly. Not everything, but that's neither here nor there. It's normal to work through one problem at a time. This doesn't work, and that sucks, so let's fix it. Flywire it. Now that doesn't work, and that sucks, so let's fix that. There are tens of problems on a new circuit court of that complexity, especially considering it was a full-on computer.

It had a screen and button inputs with LED outputs. The screen comes back from the factory, boots up, and it looks weird. There are just flipped pixels, but they're flipped by factors of four, which is obnoxious. Imagine if you were looking at your screen, and every four pixels were flipped over each other so you have almost vertical lines everywhere; everything is choppy and weird, but with thin vertical lines.

It's a little odd, but now let's take a step further, and those vertical lines are now slid over by four pixels every time, so now they're diagonal vertical lines. Very strange. Is it software? Is it hardware? What is it? At the time, I was a system architect, which meant, unfortunately, that anything that wasn't known to be software or hardware was architecture's problem because my job was to know the software, hardware, firmware, and the mechanical.

Now that obviously wasn't mechanical, so we could rule that out. So I remember we had these hanging whiteboards, and

I drew the entirety of the software-hardware interface on these boards about four feet tall, three feet wide, four of them across in this fishbowl conference room. I drew the whole thing out and stared at it.

This problem took two and a half weeks to solve going full-on with the hardware guy. One day, I was ready to give up. I was staring at these whiteboards that I'd drawn over and over and over, and the simplest thing was wrong: The memories were swapped. There were two RAM (random access memories) utilized for buffering the image, and each one buffered a few pixels. When we went to read the data out, it came out of the wrong chips, but they had put the schematic so that all the numbers were right.

There was no way to tell everything was messed up except to go back to every document, rewrite everything, and wrap your brain around the way the buses were configured in software inside the chip. But the chips were just routed wrong—they were backwards. That was the hardest thing I ever ran into and took the most effort, yet it was the simplest answer.

The egg tray.

The other challenge was the easiest one to figure out, yet the hardest to solve: the egg tray. Buttons were a problem because egg yolks would crack, and buttons would stick, and the tray would be useless. In retrospect, we should have used some form of capacitance, which is just how much charge each side can hold.

We should have used the capacitive field for these eggs to see if that would work, but we didn't. Or maybe we did. Maybe somebody vetoed it; I don't recall. Maybe it doesn't work. But we ended up using IR (infrared light) bouncing off the egg and then back down to a sensor, because it wouldn't bounce off anything if you put something black in there. It wouldn't bounce off quite as much as on a white or brown eggshell.

So we use infrared light to bounce off and come back. Awesomesauce! So we make this product, and it's great. These IR sensors are nailing it. You could tell if there's an egg in there, and we could tell if there wasn't an egg in there. Sweet.

Finally, it's time to do the real test. Let's put this in a refrigerator because that's where Americans put their eggs for some messed-up reason. Absolutely not necessary. It also makes them harder to cook and just weird. Anyway, I learned that the French don't do that, and we shouldn't too.

It was an "eggcellent" project, and I was "eggstatic" when it finally worked and "eggcited" to work on it. Egg puns aside, we put it in the fridge, and immediately, it freaks out. It can't read the eggs anymore; it's just useless. There was crackling and static. It looked like that on the graph, so we pull it back out, and it works great on the countertop again. Put it back in the fridge, and it freaks out.

Asked Google and learned that the incandescent lightbulbs in most refrigerators are quite IR noisy. They're not clean emitting bulbs at all; they have a wide spectrum of light. It's not just yellow light; it's puking every color it can possibly think of while burning tungsten out.

You think of an LED, and it has this tight, little bandwidth of light that's "perfectly" calibrated. Not perfect, but it feels calibrated compared to this crap, and then we have these incandescent bulbs just puking light.

Here we are in this situation where everybody is impacting each other because this puked light is bouncing all over and messing with all the sensors. Even with an egg in there, it's bouncing around and messing with all the sensors. It's throwing the balance off, and the hardware was tied oddly so that everything kind of leaked onto everything else, because our hardware guy wasn't the greatest. I hope he never reads this book.

He was the sweetest dude, but he was not good at what he did. He had the best degree among any of us. The rest of us were like, "I'm a ghetto kid from Detroit," "Oh, I'm a hillbilly from Tulsa," "Oh, I'm a degenerate from Germany," and then there was, "I have a PhD in electrical engineering from Carnegie Mellon" or somewhere ridiculous.

I spent weeks on this computer vision algorithm. I had to find the location of the egg tray with respect to the light in the fridge before I could do anything else. What I was looking for was a plane of light that was at an angle, but there would be some shadows depending on where you were, so the whole time, I was taking the mechanical angles of the egg tray with respect to the lightbulb into place to create a flat electrical plane across the fourteen egg cavities before I could start reading if there were eggs in there.

Frankly, it was one of the most difficult algorithms I've put on the dumbest product. It was harder than making a car drive itself, to be honest. And this was all just to detect if there was a stupid fucking egg in there.

I record all kinds of different scenarios with the actual egg tray and log it to a spreadsheet, which I turned into a matrix, and then I holed myself up in MATLAB. I worked on an algorithm consistently to get the vectors of the orientation of the egg tray, and I just wrote that core algorithm way outside of the product working with static data sets. Once the algorithm looked good, I'd port the code over to egg tray code, which was the worst Squirrel language. By the way, screw Squirrel language in its stupid ass—the worst coding language I've touched to date, and we had to use it.

It was a partnership the CEO had made—without talking to any engineers—with a chip company for hobbyists. While everybody was spending five dollars on a chip and using real adult code, we were now spending twelve dollars on a chip and using hobbyist code. That caused so many issues because now our chip's ecosystem had problems, as it was a startup, and we were a startup, and our products cost seven dollars more than they should. It was a nuisance, and the guy just kept telling me to figure it out. My job was always to figure it out; that's what I do.

In this case, it was to port the code, test it, and that's better, but not great yet. We got most of the eggs, but if you put it in that corner of the fridge, it doesn't work. So okay, get that corner of the fridge. I'll go back to the algorithm, and we just kept doing this, so I read textbooks from the '80s because they have the best AI and computer vision algorithms even before the computers could do it; they were as smart as we are today. And just go back and forth, iterate on it, change things, get the noise out, try again. Man, it was a thing. It finally worked, and I think they sold about eighty of them, and forty were returned.

V

Rocking Code and the Rock Star Life

Learning Code

The best way to learn to code is to force yourself through the gauntlet.

So you want to learn to code, or maybe you just want to live that rock star life. If you're struggling to learn code, I'd have to admit I still don't get what coding is. I find that the cheapest, dumbest, and probably the worst tutorials on the internet are the ones that have helped me the most.

School was never helpful in learning code. Back in the day, there was this series of educational books, and I read *Teach Yourself Java in 24 Hours*. I survived for about two hours. It didn't help me much, but taking apart things that already existed, looking at how that code worked, and applying it to an actual project—all that worked for me.

Saying you want to learn to code doesn't usually help because you might think that a *string* is boring or that a *character* is boring. Why do you care how many boring bits something has? But if you want to automate the LEDs in your bar so that it turns blue, green, and yellow so your liquor bottles look cool, now you've got a reason that's not boring.

However, the first thing I'd say is that YouTube is unhelpful for coding. Lots of other builds, yeah, definitely. Videos, in general, should be avoided, at least in my case. Written articles are the best because you can read forward and then go back and reread. You're not having to watch a moving target; you're able to see what the code is, copy it out, and drop it. You can skim an article in seconds; skimming a video, you always miss something.

Stackoverflow.com is the absolute best resource as any question you have will come up on that site, whether it's pasting an error or a question. For any question I have, I ask on Google and quickly look through the first ten results. Then I pop three in a new window, look for Stack Overflow as the website, and then troll them as quickly as I can.

It doesn't come down to which website, but on how quickly you can disseminate information. Start to learn which websites have the best information, and Stack Overflow is my go-to. Quora works once in a great while, but for the most part, it has fluffy answers. If you have a problem with your ear, you can go there, but if you have a problem with your code, go to Stack Overflow.

GitHub issues is another one. Sometimes you'll see GitHub issues pop up, and that's where somebody on their project has had your problem, and they talk through it as a group, which is a little different than Stack Overflow because the people know each other.

Learning coding comes down to finding what other people have done, modifying it, and putting it in your project. You don't need to reinvent the wheel, and you don't need to know how a power supply works. If you know you need five volts from the wall, buy a USB cable. You don't need to build a USB cable. What stops most people from learning code is they're trying to reinvent the wheel instead of using the pieces they need until they understand them.

Basic coding.

Many people design websites in the beginning, but I don't think that makes sense. Doing an alarm clock app on your phone or something small is a good place to start. Websites just aren't as much fun. You can't show your buddies as easily as pulling out your phone and saying, "Hey, look at what I wrote the other day." Well, you can, but it's nowhere near as clean and cool as a mobile app.

Little apps where you type and push buttons is a good place to start; make something simple and silly. One thing I did that's been fun is a little app where I speak Spanish on my phone, and it helps me get through numbers. I've been reasonably proud of it and excited for the first time in a while. I'll talk to my phone, and it runs me through all the simple numbers and simple interrogatives, and it detects the speech. It fills an actual need I had: quickly processing numbers and questions in real-life situations. I felt the other apps I was using helped me pick up the language, but not be snappy buying a coffee.

I programmed this app in Swift. I'd never programmed in Swift before, and I was able to learn it in a couple of days. I'm no expert, but I can get everything done quickly now. I wanted to learn Swift in particular because I was bored, and I like learning new languages. I like to be able to play with things. I'd done Objective-C for apps, but that's all but disappeared.

I know many languages at this point because I started learning when I was about nine years old, as if it were a hobby. The first one I learned was BASIC, and then True BASIC. There were batch files, so I learned DOS, Bash, Shell, and then I moved into C, C++, Java, JavaScript, then frameworks. There was a language called 1DC at one point, which was one-dimensional C for running processes across multiple cores. We did a 129 core processor once, so this was quite useful for image processing.

There are Squirrel language, Perl scripting, Python, now Swift. There were also Objective C, C#, and Assembly language. At one point, I did Opcode, which is ones and zeros, or machine language if you will, that you write by hand. Plus, there are a billion frameworks. Vue, React. There was a thing called QT back in the day.

The point of all of that was not to talk about how great I am, but how easily one can pick up the next coding language once you understand the basic flow of programming. It's not as important that you be perfect at a language; it's important to build things that interest you with whatever tool is best, then build the next.

Whatever excites you to build, build that, learn the correct language (or the wrong one), and then rinse and repeat. Just doing fun stuff will keep you motivated.

Example.

I had a nineteen-year-old intern last year, a construction worker who decided to go back to school. I talked to a class at the local community college to figure out who I wanted to mentor, and his eyes lit up as he was interested and asking questions. When I walked out of the class, I went to the adviser and said I wanted that kid in the front right, and he was one of three who applied.

He wasn't mentally prepared when he came in, but he had the drive; he just wasn't prepared with the math. His coding classes didn't teach him to code but to memorize words, so at first, he didn't understand what he was doing.

We decided to build a simple button-scanning matrix for his project. Starting with an internet-connected chip, he was able to talk to a server easily. Then we got to the button…

It took a reasonable amount of time to talk through coding with him, but then it came to actually writing the software, and the software is really easy. You read this way: scan the line and read a whole row, so you have to run through the columns, and then you go to the next row and run through the columns in what would be called a nested for loop, which is when you have to do the column reads, and then you have to go to the next row, again read columns.

He could not read these sixteen buttons. He'd get so frustrated, and I would draw it out on the whiteboard for him and go away and come back a few hours later, and he would have made another mess of a nightmare. So I sat with him and had him write the code on the whiteboard. I'd talk about the idea of it but then have him write the code, and I realized he was trying to solve the whole thing at once. He was trying to code through it and not break it down to its bare, smallest pieces.

What worked for him was—instead of doing these for loops—was to read all sixteen buttons one at a time and then start figuring out how to simplify that equation, which is called brute-forcing. Once he had the row iterator, his columns were still brute-forced; he was still doing four reads inside there. What could he do about that? He could turn that into a loop.

The trick that worked for him was not trying to do the elegant or proper way first, but just get it done. A lot of us, including myself, try to come up with this most elegant, efficient, wonderful solution while we sit and spin our wheels forever. Instead of running down the drag strip, we're slipping because we let the clutch out too hard. We're aiming for perfection instead of getting the job done and cleaning it up later. Just get shit done—then clean it up and be elegant and brilliant. Your job isn't to write pretty code; it's to write *working code*. Your hubris dictates it becomes pretty before it leaves your hands.

Have you ever looked at an iPhone and thought it's the most beautiful code you've ever seen? No—you look at an iPhone and think that the surface layer is great. You love what it does on the screen. You like making calls and expect the phone to work. You don't care if Apple used five lines or twenty lines or a hundred thousand lines as long as the phone works. The other programmers will give you shit, and there will be issues that fall out of sloppy coding later, but in the first run, it's not a big deal. Just don't leave that inefficient code—that's for a later book, though.

I'm not sure I would have hired him, but he did get a job in IT somewhere, and he's doing well now. I'm very proud of the kid. I've never seen somebody work through it for so long. I think that type of drive is worth more than being a brilliant math mind any day of the week.

Another example.

I mentored Wade for a long time. He was a son of the founder of a very successful record company. I never would have known that, as he didn't tell me for six or eight months that he was a rich kid; he pretended he was poor. Wade wanted to learn, and he was a smart rock star.

He went through boot camp for websites like React Native, and when he showed up, I said he was going to learn mobile apps. He said that since he went to school for six months for something completely different, he wasn't sure he could do it.

I said, "Well, I'm sure you can do it, or you can work somewhere else," because I'm shitty to work for in that way. So right away I put him in mobile, and within a few weeks, he was coming up with clever ways to make apps run by a server in the backend. He was deploying actual production things for billion-dollar companies' events within the first three weeks.

Over the next eighteen months, we worked together, and by the end, I had him working with hardware, such as building circuits, writing software for circuits, creating full apps and full websites, doing 3D printing, and using other tools. I forced this kid to go from "I make websites," to "I build cool stuff."

Now he's doing the production events for huge clients. He doesn't run a team. He prefers to build stuff, but he also likes to travel to concerts, red-carpet events, and exclusive VIP stuff.

He gets to use the software and hardware and activations as functional art pieces to meet cool people.

This kid was a super hard worker, and I put him through hell, and he came out a beast of a programmer on the other side. He figured out everything I gave him, and I'm very proud of him as he has become a more valuable developer than I'll ever be.

In engineering and coding is the one place where you are fully in control.

In the rest of the world and life, you play by other rules. When you're building something, you're in control. If it succeeds, it's you; if it fails, it's you; and I don't mean as a product. When you're building this one little thing—be it a piece of metal you want to turn into art, a circuit, or a piece of software—you are in control. There's no one to blame; there's no reason to blame. There is only you and the material, the media, whatever that is, and it's yours.

It's art, pure bliss. It's when everything else falls away. The beauty in the build is when it's only you and the media, you and the product, you and whatever it is. You're not worried about life, money, or relationships. You're one with that thing. That is the beauty, the art, and the reason to do it. The paycheck is cool, and driving stuff is fun, but building the motorcycle is cathartic.

You're either creator or consumer-biased, and if you're creator-biased, your best happy place is that beauty, that control of that one little speck of the world. Someone with a consumer bias could switch to having a creative bias. People are generally happier when they're creating rather than consuming. Consuming is easy, so you have to force yourself to attenuate that desire.

There are days when I don't want to work on anything, but when I get into it, I feel much better. It's like medicine, so you have to train yourself that if you take this medicine, you will feel better. It's so easy to sit and watch TV, but when you turn the thing on, you turn your brain off.

It's difficult to learn the constructs of coding or metalwork. There's a high point of entry, so you have to force yourself to understand that it's medicine. If you're trying to learn apps to make money, you're going to suck at it. If you're trying to learn apps because you'd rather do something with your brain than watch TV, you're probably going to be good at it. It has to be for the joy, for the music, not for the fame.

I don't think I'm proud of anything I've built. I think I did the best I could, but I don't think anything turned out as I wanted. I worked on art installations that respond to noise, and I've done lots of things along those lines, but they're cool, and they get done, but the schedules have always been so crazy that my works are never as amazing as I want them to be or as they could be.

I feel like my entire career has been constricted by schedule. I've built a lot of cool stuff, and a lot of people would be proud of it. My mom always told me I got all the things that everybody else wanted and was never stoked on them because they weren't what I wanted.

Even the job at a top tech company—that was somebody else's dream. A job with supercars, that was somebody else's dream as well. My dream has been to take the time to build something beautiful. In a perfect world, there would be nothing else. There would be no eating, no sleeping, no social interactions or social needs; there would be only the product.

For instance, the motorcycle I've been building over the past three years, I would take it all the way down to the frame and pull it all back together. Then do it again six months later. At the end of the day, it's supposed to have a dirty appeal. It's a piece of art, and that one will be probably the closest to perfect of anything I built.

I am quite proud of the motorcycle, and when she's done, she will be mean. She'll have a retro-futuristic aesthetic. I keep saying I'll be finished in a few weeks, and it's not happening. But the entire bottom end is done. I've got a little wiring left for the keyless start, and then I'll put a little RFID tag in it so you sit on it and push a button and go. Leave the key in your pocket. It'll never be done. This is the third time I've rebuilt it.

A good quote about filmmaking, which is also true for a lot of different projects, is that no film is ever completed—it's abandoned. I'm afraid that the day that I'm proud of a finished product (don't get me wrong, I'm proud of a lot of the work I've done) is the day I'll have lost my knack. And it's a concern as the more I'm willing to settle, the less I feel in tune with what I do.

Hiring Rock Stars

I work quickly, I work a ton of hours, and then I burn out, so most of my jobs are fourteen to eighteen months, and then I'm on to the next one, which keeps it interesting and fun. Employers don't like it much, but they keep hiring me. When I left one company, for example, they replaced me with seven people who couldn't keep up with deadlines, so it's sometimes hard not to be a cocky piece of shit.

I've done lots of outsourcing, as hiring people is outsourcing, so I've had a good number of employees over my career. It's only gone the way I wanted a few times, so the biggest thing I can recommend is properly vetting people for their internal fire as every time it's gone well, it's come down to the fire in the person. Ask them some technical questions to see how they think which is always important, but the bigger thing is asking them what they're excited about.

Ask them what they like to do on the weekend, and pay attention to their answers. If they're an electrical engineer, and they're excited about new ways of improving their knowledge or pushing the boundaries, you've found a good one. If they say they like to build cool stuff at home, go rock climbing, figure out how to build new gear, or daydream about ideas, you've found fire. If they mention anything that has to do with the job they do, it's positive.

Anytime you hear they like to focus on their family, that's a good person, but not necessarily the rock star you're looking for. They might be, but the odds are much lower. You certainly don't want to hear they love movies—which was said by the worst employee we ever hired. I said not to bring her on, but they hired her anyway.

When we asked what she did on the weekends, she said, "Well, I like to watch movies and hang out with friends." While this isn't a bad thing, if you're looking for rock stars, it's not a great thing to hear. I thought she'd probably be a good employee chasing a paycheck, and that's precisely what she was.

I met a guy named Matt when I hired him at a startup in New York, and he was one of the quirkiest, nerdiest guys. He was from Germany and had been in the carnival when he was young. At work, he was doing firmware and electrical engineering. He did circuit board reviews for partner-branded products, such as a wireless or a smartphone-controlled air conditioner and a smartphone-controlled power strip.

I hired him for electrical engineering, and then when I was leaving a top tech company, they offered me a job, and I declined it and recommended Matt instead. I said he was brilliant, so they gave him the job that now I wish I had taken. At his current job, he's working as an inventor. He gets to create whatever he wants to make stuff cooler. He's got some patents now on things he was fiddling around at his desk and realized something much better.

My managerial style is to find self-motivated persons and then give them a lot of challenges so they can learn by themselves. I'm looking to throw a snowball down a hill and create a massive snowball at the bottom. I'm not looking to push something up a hill or around the hill, so I want to find somebody who will start running and give them something to run to.

I don't want to micromanage as that wastes my time, and then I'm not able to do as much. I'm looking to build a team so we're all running together toward a goal. I've had a lot of good hires that come out of that same line of questioning I mentioned above, but the rock stars have charisma and are usually personable; every rock star I know is socially adept.

You can be the best technically in the world, but if you're not socially adept, you cannot be a rock star as you have to work with other people for what we do. You have to be able to interface with people to know the proper goal you're all running toward, and you must have support along the way. When you're running a marathon, you need somebody to hand you water here and there, and if you're a dick, then nobody is going to want to do that.

Wade and Matt were both good at getting support from people. They're great guys, outgoing, smiley, and make you feel good too. There's a certain leader quality in people who don't necessarily want to be leaders, and those are the people who nail it. They don't want to be CEO, but everybody is willing to follow them because it's going to be a good time. You're going to be working while you do it, but it's going to be fun. It's the Tom Sawyer thing: let's paint this fence—it'll be fun.

You can mess up and be a fuckup, but you can still turn out well.

Wade was a college dropout who had been cut off monetarily by his family. He made his way back by being stoked on building cool stuff.

My buddy in Florida was from a poor family. His dad was an out-of-work baker, and I believe his mom was a nurse, and his brother was a fuckup. They lived in a small house, and while he didn't have many hopes for life, he's now a retired multimillionaire.

After college, my buddy Matt partied for months in Spain and now works at one of the biggest companies in the world in a great position.

I have a buddy with a spot in the Santa Cruz Mountains. No idea how he got that, but he drinks profusely, plays poker, and runs an engineering team. He's also a multimillionaire from startup stuff.

The guy who founded one of the bigger cryptocoins is a complete asshat, douchebag, multi-multi-multimillionaire from San Francisco. He's a completely gross human being but still doing well for himself. Although he's not somebody I would look up to, he proves my point that you can be a total fuckup and still do well.

I used to have a ski lease in Lake Tahoe with about ten or twelve people from work. We'd go skiing on the weekends. After I left that job was probably the first time I ran into a bunch of them at the ski lease, and the whole time I worked with them, I hid the fact that I smoked weed, and nobody else said anything either. It turns out we all smoked weed, and nobody told anybody else. Oops.

It was this big eye-opening moment that we were all privately partying like rock stars yet hiding it from the others. As I've gone further in my career, I've found that startup life is pure hedonism. We work crazy hours, do crazy drugs, drink our faces off, ruin our bodies, but then ride bicycles or go rock climbing. It's a fast-paced, never-stop hedonism.

It's safe to say that more people than you would expect are living like rock stars. Even the kids from Stanford are living like rock stars. Nobody's proper. We put on our proper faces, but we're getting worse at it. Now people wear shorts at work.

I dated the CEO of a company that was valued at $300 million or so, and that girl could drink me under the table every time. Plus, she loved her punk and metal almost more than I did. She was a biker chick at home, and then she'd get ready for work, and she was prim and proper at the office. She did yoga and went on runs. She was an amazing woman.

But damn, the girl went too hard. We dated briefly and I, unfortunately, ruined that because she reminded me of my stepmom, which threw me off in the worst ways. That girl was a rock star, and I miss hanging out with her.

I also dated (or hung out with) the CEO of a marketing campaign startup that has maybe twenty-three employees and is doing well, and that girl partied. And when I say party, I mean she *partied hard*. She hung out frequently with a friend of ours who was a reality-TV-show star, so she'd be between Nashville and crazy countries with him. She kept moving, kept rocking, living that life.

My buddy Rickie owned an eco-lodge hotel and a brand that was to span multiple countries, but he lost the second hotel deal last year. This guy was so outgoing. He was in real estate, and he did over half a billion in transactions in Canada and then said he was sick of being in a suit. He left and opened this hotel down in Central America that became the place where famous artists would record albums. He opened this hotel so he could party with famous people, get down, and surf every day. He does ayahuasca ceremonies and has a full-on hippie face, yet he's a devious businessman underneath.

I have another friend who's running for mayor of a small town in Colorado. He owns an antique hotel that he's flipped into a nice boutique hotel. I've never seen anybody in my life take more mushrooms and dive into sea urchin-filled, crystal-clear waters. He used to be a lawyer in New York and then decided he wanted to be a ski bum but then opened the hotel. This guy is amazing. He was prim and proper most of the time, and then I saw him come up to me with eyes like plates, and he gave me the biggest hug and ran away. This man is super successful and awesome, and he's in the process of opening a whole chain of hotels at this point.

Is the rock star lifestyle helpful, or is it destructive? Looking at today's society, my opinion is that today is the right time to be a rock star. Historically, there were times it was not. We don't carry ourselves like we used to. There are no airs about what we do and don't do; we don't hide our skeletons. All the heroes on the TV are confessing to the worst things they've ever done. For example, 50 Cent was a gang member. Every popular song on the radio right now is about codeine and drugs.

We air our dirty laundry these days, so it's more acceptable to party, and it's almost a rite of passage to live that startup life. There are a lot of people that don't, and there are a lot of industries that don't accept it. For example, the automotive industry isn't a place you're going to advertise the fact that you do drugs because it's an old-fashioned industry.

You're not going to work at IBM or Apple and do crazy drugs. You're expected to carry yourself appropriately at those places. It's a different world. It's the traveler outside of the mainstream. It's not the monster.com jobs, buy a house, have kids, and live that lifestyle.

Today, it's the move to be young, have fun, and maybe you're in your thirties, but you're not dead. Most of the startup CEOs I've met in my career, and most of the executives and people you'd consider successful, have this party life that they maintain. You have to have a lot of money to live like that, so you have to be driven. But you don't want to be working all the time, so you're going to work as hard, as fast, and as well as you can so it doesn't come back to bite you in the ass next week.

That used to motivate me, but at this point, I don't feel the need to party anymore. I haven't drunk, smoked, or put anything in my body for five weeks. My life is bland, though it's uniquely boring. But boring is good sometimes. I'm trying to figure out the next stage of life and do that clearheaded and then probably go back to partying too hard because you never stop doing that, you just take breaks here and there to detox.

Handling Clients

There are lots of particularly tricky clients, as that's what a client tends to be. I never think I've done well enough, but the biggest thing is to keep calm and set boundaries. At work, I've trained myself to smile more the angrier I get. Do that, or you get an angry face. When dealing with clients, they need to feel in charge, but you have to set boundaries.

Keep the relationship alive. You can be right, but if they don't like you, they'll get rid of you even if you're right. Make sure the client likes you, for lack of a better way to put it. You can pretend like it's business all day, but it's not; it's high school.

I've had a couple of situations where I haven't delivered the greatest product. It wasn't fully my fault, but I did agree to do it within a certain time frame, and my product wasn't my proudest moment. However, the feedback has generally been, "Everybody here loves you. Let's do better next time."

"Are you kidding me? I failed miserably. Why would you hire us?"

"Well, we like you and we like working with you."

But it doesn't always go well, and sometimes it comes to a head. Last year, I lost my mind, and for the first time in my life, I yelled at a client. It was absolutely necessary, and they are still causing me headaches. They've hit me up every day this week to fix something not under warranty, but they haven't paid me since last July, so I have to keep being nice to them. They owe me over six figures, so what am I going to do? Next week, the lawyer talks to him, so that's the next phase.

How to determine if you're the right person for the job?

I don't care if I get the job or not; I don't care if I win the bid or not. That's been the first step for me in winning these jobs. But I've always focused on enjoying what I do, and I suppose clients can see the fire. What I've learned is that if you can speak intelligently, people are less interested in your degree, GPA, and work experience. They want to know about these things, but that's it.

When I was hired at on particularly large company, I put sentence fragments under all the jobs I had before on my resume. Instead of the big bulleted list detailing how I managed a team, I stated I built a firmware architecture. On my LinkedIn page, I have short job descriptions, yet I get offers all the time. I don't care to tell them what I've done; I want to talk about what they want to talk about. If they talk about the project or their technology, then I ask them questions about what they do and interject things.

When I was young, I interviewed with a headphone company, and they said that the reason they hired me was due to one question. I asked them about their products, and when the interviewer discussed the actual product, I asked, "For your potentiometers, are you using linear taper or logarithmic?"

What got me hired was number 1, I actively asked questions about the product, but number 2, I asked a question that showed I understood their product. For a linear pot, you would use a digital system, and in a logarithmic, you would use an analog, and I was probing to see what type or what style of circuits they use to learn if they were old school or new school.

When we were talking about the set of headphones, I was trying to build it in my head the way I would build it. I asked questions about what they did to see how they built it and tried to get into their product. I wasn't concerned with the job—I was concerned with the product. I've always asked about the company and the product and the team.

Furthermore, I'll inquire as to the demeanor of the team. Do the people hang out after work? How late do people stay there, generally? What time does the workday start? Do they have activities they do together?

I like to hear that they play soccer or ride bikes because I get the dynamic of how the team interacts. Professional is cool, but things don't move quickly that way, and in high-stress environments, if you aren't more than coworkers, you're screwed. I have asked those kinds of questions in all my interviews since I was about twenty-four years old.

The culture of a place is important to me. It's a big part of my life because it's most of my life, and I don't want it to suck. I hated my first internship that turned into my first job. The people sucked, and they were so boring that I thought if I was going to spend this much time at work, I'd rather work at McDonald's with cool people and free McNuggets than make a billion dollars with assholes.

At one startup, I was working with my friends, and we were having fun and drinking our faces off. I clicked with the people. I talked to one guy about the skateboard company he ran on the side. Another guy and I got deep into the nerdy stuff we built at home and our love for Linux. I eventually lived with two of those guys after we all left that company.

When I interviewed, it was with the entire team I'd work with, and it was an all-day affair. They made it a social day by giving me a half-hour with each person, and then we all had lunch together, and we all clicked. I've spoken with three of those people in the past week, and it was six years ago that I did this interview. That was the interview that nailed it. Since then, everything's been rather fluid.

Networking helps build your career.

Networking is the best way to find a job. You're probably not going to get a reasonable job from the internet, but you're going to get good jobs from people you know from places you've been. Get your foot in the door, and be close to that industry however you can. Go to meetups and events, and take an internship even if you're forty. You can be known as a giant asshole, which I might be, but as long as you're known for being able to have fun, speak intelligently, deliver, and good at what you do, you'll always be employed unless you want nothing to do.

My mom set up my first internship when I was nineteen. She called a company she worked with and said, "Hey, my son's smart." (Remember to let other people say you're smart.) So my first internship was when I was working in automotive while attending a community college. She brought me in for three months because she couldn't find a good intern. She told them I'd been coding since I was nine, and although I was in art school, I could do the work.

I did field validation software in C code for body control modules for cars. I had no idea what I was doing, yet I made it work and made it work quickly. Following that, she set me up with one of the companies she worked with to do an internship, and from there, I took over.

That next internship led to my first contracting job. One of the managers there called me and said, "I remember when you were an intern, and you were great. Do you want to come work for me as an engineer now that you're done with school?" Then one of the guys across the cubicle from me at that job pulled me into the next job working on the supercars.

The company I started after that stint got work from a guy I met while working on supercars. He was a contractor there, and then when he had another gig, he said, "Hey, I remember when you were running the team there. You want to do this with me?"

Then I got the call to work for the headphone company. They got their hands on my resume through a network of people. I think my mom gave it to one of the initial developers of the iPad or the iPhone, and it got around Silicon Valley, which resulted in that call. That was the interview where I dropped the question: "What potentiometer are you using?"

I don't know how the next startup got my name, but they randomly called me out of the blue one day. I didn't apply and didn't ask; they called me. It was the same with the tech giant:

they contacted me as they were trying to steal the startup's engineers. From the next job, I met one of the employees at an airport, wrote an app for his company, and then they eventually gave me part of their company.

From there, I got jobs through people I met in my travels who I worked with and jobs through people I knew. Everything is interrelated; nothing has resulted from me cold-calling. My entire career has been a result of calling a buddy if I need something or being reached out to and open to opportunities.

I believe it's because I'm focused on the work and the people. I'm not focused on the job, the paycheck, or the title. I'm focused on building, and I feel that's what made me a better builder because I'm not diverting my brain space and abilities toward this whole sociopolitical mess. Instead, I'm just building cool shit with cool people.

The End...for Now

I almost find the word engineer offensive: it's a job, not a person.

An inventor is a person, and engineering is a job. All the great engineers I can think of were inventors or artists, and engineering is something they did in the process of creating. You can have a knack for engineering, and that knack is important. An example of a great engineer who was also an artist is Da Vinci as he engineered while he was inventing and dreaming. Tesla engineered while being a great scientist and inventor.

Engineering is a tool in the toolbox, like painting or anything else. I don't think an engineer is what you are; it's a job. I don't think anybody would say they were born to be a front desk clerk; they're paying their bills as a front desk clerk while they are a musician or some other kind of creative.

I would love to sit down with Feynman, have a drink, and listen to him tell stories because it sounds like he's a much better storyteller than I am. I would want the stories he didn't put in his books, the dirty ones. I know there are dirty ones out there with an attitude like that, and just being such a smiley, happy, funny guy, there's got to be a lot of borderline things he did that he couldn't write about in the '80s.

I would like to speak with Oppenheimer about his thought process. I would be interested to know how he felt. He was a patriot, but at the same time, he knew what he was up to, and I'd be interested in learning about his morality on the situation. Because I mean we've all read the Patriot's side.

To be totally cliché, I'd love to sit down with Tesla, but I would want to talk to him in his older age when he was going insane. I'd want to know what it's like and make sure it's something I can prepare for and avoid. I've spent months alone in the desert now, and I'm starting to lose my mind. I'd like to see if that's what happens or if there's a way out of insanity. You can only live with your projects and avoid people for so long, and then it starts to wear on you.

I'd love to talk to him about that because obviously everything else he did was brilliant or insane—probably both. I'd like to see the fallout of that kind of lifestyle because I know that party people turn happy and older and burn out in other ways. But you don't see the recluse as much, and you don't see what they become.

I want to work on projects that make the world a better place.

This is a big problem I have had my entire career. When I was young, I wanted to help people, and I don't feel that anything I've built helps people. You can always argue that by creating better consumer products, you're lowering the cost of devices and research for medical, which helps people.

But that's a very long thread to pull. We're creating landfill fodder and driving consumerism, and while there's a difference to be made, I don't think I've done it yet. I think I've put a lot of crap in your pockets and in your cars and made a lot out of products for rich pricks. I've worked on all kinds of high-end luxury products, but I haven't helped humanity.

Most of us aren't furthering society; I don't think we're doing good things. Questions we all ask ourselves should include, "What are we doing all of this for?" Are we creating more trash for landfills? Are we driving consumerism? Or are we helping people create a better life? Are we just doing mental gymnastics?

I did mental gymnastics for years in saying I'm driving medical, by arguing with myself that I'm lowering the costs of products. I'm not, but I can be. I learned a lot, so maybe all this was for a better future; maybe I had to learn on the consumer side so I could create better medical devices or clean water.

Often you don't think about unintended consequences because you're in it, but as I step away from my builds, I see things that are bothersome, such as the amount of trash we're creating is impossible to recycle. How are you going to recycle a lithium battery with any efficiency?

We are so focused on consumerism and money as opposed to making people's lives better. We aren't trying to create products that enhance lives. We are trying to create products that make a few people rich.

Technology is giving us more information and educating us, but it can also misinform and easily lie to us, which is dangerous. My biggest sadness is the laziness I see coming out of this time. People are less in tune with the world. We've become so service-oriented that most people who own a car don't even know how to change a tire.

We're becoming helpless in the process of learning how to be better at clicking buttons, so we're getting better at understanding the user interface and worse at understanding our world. We don't know which plants to eat if the power goes out. Technology is creating a helpless species and, frankly speaking, ruining the place on which we live.

It's like farting in a closed room. What a bad idea, but that's what we've been doing. We have one earth, and we're constantly farting in it. We've done a lot of procrastination, and there's going to be a time where technology is going to have to shift, but first, it's going to have to get worse for the masses.

At some point, people won't be able to afford to buy phones. And the trash will be piled up so high that our lives will become terrible across the board except for a select few. Once that gap splits hard enough, the resources thin enough, then we'll end up in another revolution that's driven by making our lives better.

In original America, people wanted to split from Britain to make their lives better. It wasn't about corporate; it wasn't about getting another car; it was about living free or dying. That was a pure time. Now we're living in the age that worried Abe Lincoln: corporations are taking over, and they own everything, and we are funneling money toward certain people.

Once everything breaks down, we will have a renaissance again, and that'll be awesome. I don't know what those inventions will be, but I feel they will be targeted toward cleaning the air, water, and environment, and taking care of our bodies. We will need to clean up the damage that all these things are doing to us.

Eventually, we have to turn off the TVs. When that happens, people won't be happy anymore. I believe that the future of technology will be to clean up our mess and make less of it. Once there's a big enough need, I feel we can all get together.

Crowdfunding health products would be amazing. Imagine if everybody in America threw a dollar toward crowdfunding a glucose monitor so they could cost $20 and $1 for the refills? We could pull together $338 million. We could ruin the big corporations with nonprofit tech companies if they were crowdfunded.

My biggest gripe about healthcare is the cost. Mylan was charging $600 for two EpiPens that cost them about $7 to make. With a healthy distribution supply chain, you could sell them for $25 at a massive profit, and then more people with allergies could afford them. But it's disgusting what we permit our countries to do. I propose we crowdfund medical nonprofit companies where the CEO doesn't make $18 million a year in bonuses.

If I had to give up coding and engineering, I would open an ice cream stand. When I was younger, I wanted to open a bar on the beach, but that's not always the happiest place. I want to open an ice cream stand in Central America and make everybody happy. It's okay. I'm lactose intolerant; I won't get diabetes from running it.

However, the biggest change I want to make in my life is to make a change. I don't know what that change is, but I can tell you at the moment I am not happy sitting in the desert doing nothing. Retirement was fun for a few months. Now it's not so much fun.

My vision for my future.

When I was growing up, my grandfather always said, "I never had a plan, son. I woke up and did my best at whatever God put in front of me that day." I like to think of that as life surfing, and that's what I've done my whole life, yet I keep trying to plan, and it makes me miserable. My only plan is to continue to sit on the board and wait for a pretty wave and ride that pretty wave until it breaks on the shore and then swim back out and catch the next pretty wave and see what happens.

Now, on those waves, I'm going to guide left and right. I'm going to choose which waves look pretty and glassy enough to ride. I don't want to take the choppy ones, and I don't want the ones that can break on me, but aside from that, I'm going to keep surfing.

Honestly, I don't know if I'm going to stay sober. If I like being sober, I'm going to stay sober. If I don't like it, I'm going to stop. My process is purely qualitative. It is all about the feelings, but it's not based on one day. I will give it about a month and see how I feel overall. I will put the plan out there and wait.

When I was young, I liked tattoos, so I got tattoos. But first, I would draw my tattoo and put it in a book and wait six months. If in six months I still wanted it, I would get the tattoo. I regret none of my tattoos, and I'm not mad about them, but I'm not sure I would get them again. I made sure not to get any visible ones, and now there are no rooms I'd want to be in where I wouldn't be allowed to have tattoos.

I've had a lot of failures, but I don't feel bad about them, and I don't regret any of my dumb decisions. There are a lot of things I could have done better, but then, I wouldn't have had rad experiences. I could have looked for a job at a place like Apple or Amazon and had a great time, but instead, I tried living in Nicaragua and Lisbon, traveled for a year, came out to the desert, and lost my mind.

Someone important once wrote a book called *It's All Made Up,* which is what none of us are told growing up. Every single thing we're doing is about people making things up. One person has an idea, and then other people follow that person. There's no magic: corporations are just people full of people. It's a bunch of kids in a sandbox, and one kid says, "I'm the king of the sandbox. This is how it works."

That structure applies to the law, the taxes, and everything else. I realized that people don't know more than me after I left that corporate world. When I was in Nicaragua, I realized I was still waking up every morning. I hadn't had a job in months, and without a job, without a career plan or past. I wasn't dead.

It was pretty rad, and I came to realize that all these things I'd come to believe were made up so that I would buy more crap I didn't need. I didn't need to pay for a car to get to work because I didn't need to go to work, for example. You get locked into these belief systems, and then you realize you can make money. Money comes. You can find it; you don't have to have somebody hand you a paycheck. It's much easier to get a paycheck, but somebody at the top went out and found money and shared it with all you.

See, it's all made up.

***

These are my opinions, sometimes conflicting, sometimes flat-out bad. Thank you for your money and time in exchange for my platitudinous rant.

About the Author

Paul W. Carter is a fiction shaped like a man, running around anonymously to commit gonzo coding - and to inflict this memoir upon you. If you could find him—which you can't—he could be found coding from shipping containers, bumming around tropical locales, and pursuing life wherever his fancy (not to mention questionable substances) takes him.